CW00552271

# *Penguin Monarchs*

## THE HOUSES OF WESSEX AND DENMARK

| | |
|---|---|
| Athelstan | Tom Holland |
| Aethelred the Unready | Richard Abels |
| Cnut | Ryan Lavelle |
| Edward the Confessor | James Campbell |

## THE HOUSES OF NORMANDY, BLOIS AND ANJOU

| | |
|---|---|
| William I | Marc Morris |
| William II | John Gillingham |
| Henry I | Edmund King |
| Stephen | Carl Watkins |
| Henry II | Richard Barber |
| Richard I | Thomas Asbridge |
| John | Nicholas Vincent |

## THE HOUSE OF PLANTAGENET

| | |
|---|---|
| Henry III | Stephen Church |
| Edward I | Andy King |
| Edward II | Christopher Given-Wilson |
| Edward III | Jonathan Sumption |
| Richard II | Laura Ashe |

## THE HOUSES OF LANCASTER AND YORK

| | |
|---|---|
| Henry IV | Catherine Nall |
| Henry V | Anne Curry |
| Henry VI | James Ross |
| Edward IV | A. J. Pollard |
| Edward V | Thomas Penn |
| Richard III | Rosemary Horrox |

## THE HOUSE OF TUDOR

| | |
|---|---|
| Henry VII | Sean Cunningham |
| Henry VIII | John Guy |
| Edward VI | Stephen Alford |
| Mary I | John Edwards |
| Elizabeth I | Helen Castor |

## THE HOUSE OF STUART

| | |
|---|---|
| James I | Thomas Cogswell |
| Charles I | Mark Kishlansky |
| [Cromwell | David Horspool] |
| Charles II | Clare Jackson |
| James II | David Womersley |
| William III & Mary II | Jonathan Keates |
| Anne | Richard Hewlings |

## THE HOUSE OF HANOVER

| | |
|---|---|
| George I | Tim Blanning |
| George II | Norman Davies |
| George III | Amanda Foreman |
| George IV | Stella Tillyard |
| William IV | Roger Knight |
| Victoria | Jane Ridley |

## THE HOUSES OF SAXE-COBURG & GOTHA AND WINDSOR

| | |
|---|---|
| Edward VII | Richard Davenport-Hines |
| George V | David Cannadine |
| Edward VIII | Piers Brendon |
| George VI | Philip Ziegler |
| Elizabeth II | Douglas Hurd |

RICHARD BARBER

# Henry II

## A Prince Among Princes

ALLEN LANE
*an imprint of*
PENGUIN BOOKS

ALLEN LANE

UK | USA | Canada | Ireland | Australia
India | New Zealand | South Africa

Allen Lane is part of the Penguin Random House group of companies
whose addresses can be found at global.penguinrandomhouse.com.

First published 2015
001

Copyright © Richard Barber, 2015

The moral right of the author has been asserted

Set in 9.5/13.5 pt Sabon LT Std
Typeset by Jouve (UK), Milton Keynes
Printed in Great Britain by Clays Ltd, St Ives plc

ISBN: 978-0-141-97708-9

www.greenpenguin.co.uk

Penguin Random House is committed to a
sustainable future for our business, our readers
and our planet. This book is made from Forest
Stewardship Council® certified paper.

# Contents

## HENRY II

*For Gay*

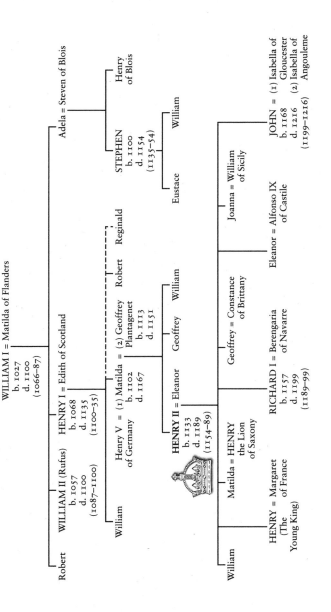

WILLIAM I = Matilda of Flanders
b. 1027
d. 1100
(1066–87)

Robert

WILLIAM II (Rufus)
b. 1057
d. 1100
(1087–1100)

William

HENRY I = Edith of Scotland
b. 1068
d. 1135
(1100–35)

Henry V = (1) Matilda = (2) Geoffrey Plantagenet
of Germany      b. 1102      b. 1113
                d. 1167      d. 1151

Reginald

Robert

Adela = Steven of Blois

Henry
of Blois

STEPHEN
b. 1100
d. 1154
(1135–54)

Eustace          William

HENRY II = Eleanor
b. 1133
d. 1189
(1154–89)

Geoffrey          William

William

HENRY = Margaret
(The         of France
Young King)

Matilda = HENRY
the Lion
of Saxony

RICHARD I = Berengaria
b. 1157      of Navarre
d. 1199
(1189–99)

Geoffrey = Constance
of Brittany

Joanna = William
of Sicily

Eleanor = Alfonso IX
of Castile

JOHN = (1) Isabella of
b. 1168      Gloucester
d. 1216   (2) Isabella of
(1199–1216)   Angouleme

**N**

| | |
|---|---|
| | lands inherited by Henry |
| | lands acquired by marrying Eleanor in 1152 |
| | lands acquired by Henry after 1154 |
| | overlordships acquired by Henry after 1154 |

*North Sea*

Aberdeen

Edinburgh

Carlisle

Durham

Armagh

York

Dublin

Chester

Cork

Bristol

London

Southampton

*English Channel*

Rouen

Caen

Avranches

Paris

ATLANTIC
OCEAN

Domfront

Le Mans

Angers

Tours

Nantes

Poitiers

| 0 | 200 miles |
|---|---|
| 0 | 400 km |

Bordeaux

Bayonne

Toulouse

# The Domains of Henry Plantagenet

# Henry II

# I

# The Man

'I saw King Henry, many times. Yet I still remember the first time I encountered him and looked at him: and I knew at once this was a man I would not forget. He was very handsome, with a face that men and women never tired of looking at, however often they had already seen him; his complexion was freckled, and his grey eyes were set off by his close-cropped tawny hair. He was usually calm, but if something angered him, his look would suddenly become fierce; his face flushed red, while his eyes became bloodshot. His head was large and round, with a short neck. He was only of middling height, and yet seemed taller than he was, for he always wore a short cloak, unlike other Normans – hence his nickname "Curtmantle". He was well built, of good proportions, and sound in wind and limb, agile and energetic, with broad shoulders and sturdy limbs: he had extraordinary stamina. He was bow-legged from riding, and had the powerful shins of a man who spent his life in the saddle. Naturally corpulent, he had a large stomach; to avoid becoming too fat, he was careful to eat and drink in moderation. To keep himself fit, he adopted a harsh physical regime for the same reason.

'As he grew older, his hair began to turn grey, and his habit of riding all day and then standing whenever he was in public – whether at Mass, in council or transacting the business of the kingdom – caused his legs to swell, and he suffered badly from an ingrowing toenail. His endless life on horseback meant that he was often kicked by horses and injured himself by frequently spurring on recalcitrant animals. In fact, although he kept himself fit, he did not trouble about the care of his body in other ways: he only wore gloves when hawking, and his hands were rough as a result. He dressed simply, without any regard to fashion: his boots were plain, his caps had no decoration, and his clothes were light and practical – this was his reason for wearing a short riding cloak at all times. Royal splendour was not his style, though he exuded a royal dignity in his simple garments.

'When war or the business of state required it, he would cover huge distances on horseback each day, distances which would have entailed four or five days' journey for an ordinary traveller. He was restless in the extreme: even when he was out hunting, he would leave at crack of dawn, riding through forests and wastelands, and scaling hills and mountains in pursuit of his quarry. He never lingered in his palaces, but endlessly travelled up and down his domains.

'His imposing physical presence was matched by an equally imposing intellect. Languages were no obstacle to him, and he knew something of most of the tongues spoken in the Christian world, though he only used Latin and French. He read widely, but his particular interest was in matters of law and government rather than the new romances favoured by his wife and sons. He had a keen and

enquiring mind: in his household, every day was like a
school, and there was constant discussion of difficult ques-
tions. Henry would often gather his officials around him to
try to disentangle some point of law or problem of administration. He was the most learned of kings, even more so
than William I of Sicily, who had Peter of Blois as his tutor.

'When he had to give judgement in a lawsuit, his decisions were always admirable, and he was a subtle and wise
thinker when faced with difficult cases. His passion was
the establishment of peace and justice within his realms.
He worked tirelessly to achieve this, summoning councils,
making laws and, on his travels, investigating the actions of
the justices he had appointed. He began his reign by declaring that he would restore the laws of his grandfather Henry
I, but as time went on, he devised many new and just legal
procedures.

'I often heard him speak, in his hoarse, cracked voice; he
was eloquent on formal occasions, at councils and in law
courts, and in private discussions. In everyday conversation
he was approachable and friendly, full of wit and charm.
Despite the throng of people who surrounded him, he never
once forgot anyone with whom he had been in close contact, and he could always recall things worth remembering
which he had been told. So he had at his fingertips both a
ready knowledge of nearly the whole of history and also
practical experience of almost everything in daily affairs.

'The only thing that could turn him aside on his ceaseless
travels was the prospect of good hawking or hunting, for
falconry was one of his passions. Otherwise, he was imper-
vious to the discomforts of the journey. These discomforts

were all too keenly felt by me and his other companions and by the court at large, as we followed him pell-mell on long days on the road; he moved as fast as a royal courier with urgent messages, and frequently changed his mind. If the king promised to remain in a place for that day, he was sure to upset all the arrangements by departing early in the morning. As a result, you would see men dashing around as if they were mad, beating their pack-horses, running their carts into one another – in short, giving a lively imitation of Hell. At the end of the day, things were no better: the king would suddenly turn aside before the agreed destination, and find somewhere to lodge, leaving us to fend for ourselves. I hardly dare say it, but I believe in truth he took a delight in seeing what a fix he put us in. After wandering some three or four miles in an unknown wood, in the dark, we thought ourselves lucky if we stumbled upon some filthy little hovel in which to sleep. There was often an argument about a mere hut, and swords were drawn over a lodging that pigs would have shunned.

'This restlessness worked to his advantage, however, in matters of war. Because he could cover in one day what his enemies would consider a march of four or five days, he was always able to surprise them by his sudden appearance. War was for him a last resort, and he would negotiate until he had exhausted all possible solutions rather than embark on a campaign. In the field, he was expert in encouraging his men. If a castle was regarded as impregnable, he would take it in a few days, because of his enthusiasm and skill in organizing his troops.

'I never saw him sit down except when he was at table or in the saddle. Yet I found him as often with a book in his hands as a hunting bow; he was as passionate about learning as about hunting. And in public he was approachable; I watched him being pushed and pulled here and there by the crowd of suitors without complaint. He would even hear state business when at Mass. Yet once he was in his private chamber, he would not tolerate disturbance.

'In short, Henry did nothing in a proud or overbearing fashion. Sober, modest, pious, true to his word, he was prudent, generous and victorious; always ready to honour those who deserved it.'

This portrait of Henry is drawn largely from that of Walter Map, who knew the king from the beginning of his reign in England in 1154 until Henry's death in 1189. Other details come from the description of Henry sent to the Archbishop of Palermo in 1177 by Peter of Blois, another of his courtiers and a great scholar. Another source is the writings of Gerald of Wales, who seems to have admired and hated Henry in equal measure – Gerald never forgave him for refusing to ratify his election as Bishop of St David's in 1176, but none the less entered his service some years later. The remarkably detailed descriptions that we have confirm Walter Map's account of the deep impression he made on those who encountered him.[1]

In letters and chronicles, there are eyewitness accounts of Henry in action, which confirm and enlarge on these direct descriptions of him. Henry disliked pomp and ceremony, and it seems that when he appointed Thomas Becket, a clerk of relatively humble origin, as his chancellor, one of the things that he expected Becket to do was to maintain an impressive retinue and household as the king's representative, so that Henry himself did not have to involve himself in such outward show. Becket enjoyed this role, and when he went to Paris in 1157 to negotiate a marriage between King Louis's daughter Margaret and Henry's young son Henry, he travelled in the utmost splendour 'so that the person of his liege lord might be honoured in his envoy',[2] with twenty-four changes of clothing, silk garments to be given away, every kind of fur, and cloaks and carpets as well. Eight waggons, each with a fearsome guard dog, and with monkeys mounted on the horses, carried his baggage; and twelve packhorses were needed for the silver and plate for his table. Henry, by contrast, came separately, with a small entourage and no display of riches. The king used to tease Becket – who obviously loved such trappings – about his delight in rich dress: as they rode through London one day, Henry saw an old man in a ragged coat and suggested to Becket that it would be an act of charity to give him a cloak. 'Yes,' said Becket, 'you, as king, should see to it.' At this, Henry took hold of Becket's splendid cape and, after a short tussle, pulled it off and gave it to the old man. William Fitzstephen, Becket's biographer, who tells this story, comments on how 'when the daily round of business had been dealt with, the king and Thomas would sport together, like boys of the same age, in hall, in church and out riding together'.[3]

An episode from the very end of his reign shows that Henry retained a keen sense of humour. Bishop Hugh of

Avalon had deeply angered Henry by excommunicating one of his foresters, and was summoned to the king's hunting lodge at Woodstock to explain himself. Henry saw him coming, and in a fury rode off into the forest followed by Bishop Hugh, where he and his barons dismounted and sat round in a circle. Not a word was spoken, and to pass the time, Henry called for needle and thread and began to sew up a leather bandage covering an injured finger. After a while, Hugh remarked quietly, 'How like your cousins of Falaise you are!' To the courtiers' amazement, the king burst out laughing and rolled on the ground. When he came to himself, he explained that William the Conqueror had been a bastard, and his mother was said to have been the daughter of one of the leather workers for which the town of Falaise was famous. The bishop was duly forgiven.[4]

There was, however, another side to his character, noted by his enemies: an uncontrollable temper. John of Salisbury reported an incident in 1166, when Henry was in his thirties, over a knight who spoke in favour of the King of Scotland, with whom Henry had just quarrelled, describing how 'the king, flying into his usual temper, flung his cap from his head, pulled off his belt, threw off his cloak and clothes, grabbed the silken coverlet off the couch, and sitting as it might be on a dung heap started chewing pieces of straw'.[5] Opposition frequently roused him to fury, and this became a constant theme in his struggle with Thomas Becket; he felt that Becket, whom he had raised first to be Chancellor of England and then Archbishop of Canterbury, had betrayed him by his constant insistence on the Church's rights and the Church's law. Their later meetings were often bad-tempered, and

Henry veered from appeals to their old friendship while Becket had been chancellor, to angry reproaches. In one such moment, he swore never to exchange the kiss of peace with Becket, and this was to lead to the archbishop's return to England without the surety of the king's favour that such a ceremony would have implied. And when Henry heard false rumours that Becket was in open rebellion against him, at the head of troops ravaging the countryside, he responded by declaring that his courtiers were 'all traitors who could not summon up the zeal and loyalty to rid him of the harassment of one man'.[6] This was the trigger for the events that led to the archbishop's martyrdom.

The fact is that Henry was genuinely pious, but religion took second place to the cares of government. Gerald of Wales accused him of confounding the laws of Church and state, 'out of zeal for justice', and usurping 'the things that pertained to God'. Towards the end of his life, he took a vow to go on crusade; while the enthusiasm was genuine, as with so many would-be royal crusaders of the period, politics and affairs of state would probably have prevented him from going if his death had not done so.

Concern for his subjects lay behind Henry's zeal for justice; this same concern also showed itself in his liberality to his servants and to those in distress. Even Gerald of Wales admits that he was 'liberal beyond compare in almsgiving'.[7] While another chronicler records how Henry, early in his reign, 'changed the ancient and inhuman custom with regard to those shipwrecked, and ordered that those who were rescued should be treated humanely, prescribing heavy penalties for anyone who molested them or plundered their goods'.[8] Walter Map tells of an occasion when the king crossed from Normandy in ships provided by the ports of the south coast as their feudal duty. The fleet was overwhelmed by a storm, and only Henry's ship reached port; the rest were wrecked or stranded. The next day, the king sent for the seamen and shipowners and compensated them for their losses, even though he was not required to do so, and large sums were involved.[9] Faced with a famine in Anjou and Maine in 1176, Henry opened the storehouses on his estates there to feed the poor. These were public acts: Walter Map says that he often also gave alms in secret.

Henry was consistent in his friendship: he hardly ever changed his mind about someone – 'whom he had once hated he scarcely ever loved, but whom he had once loved he scarcely ever called to mind with hatred'.[10] The one thing that Henry could not abide was betrayal, and it was the feeling that those closest to him – his wife and sons, his erstwhile friend Thomas Becket – had broken faith with him that led to the great disasters of his reign. He never forgave Becket. With his sons, he alternated between fury and forgiveness, unable to trust them or to find a way of working with them. Gerald of Wales eloquently sums up the resulting distress: 'He found strife instead of safety, ruin instead of repose, ingratitude instead of constancy, and the utmost confusion instead of peace and tranquillity.'[11] The peace and justice he had sought for others, he could not find for himself.

When Henry came to the throne in 1154, aged twenty-one, the Norman kingdom in England was less than a century old, and he was separated from William the Conqueror by only two generations. William had been succeeded by two of his sons, and the connection between England and Normandy was by no means automatic after 1066; he had intended his eldest son, Robert Curthose, to inherit Normandy, and his second son, William Rufus, to have England. But Robert lacked his father's energy and sound judgement, and was unenthusiastic about the business of ruling his duchy: he went on crusade in 1096, having leased Normandy to William Rufus. William Rufus died while Robert was on the way back to Normandy and his younger brother Henry seized the crown. When Robert reached the duchy, the political situation deteriorated. His barons rebelled; Henry I supported them, and Robert was captured in 1106. He spent the next twenty-eight years in fairly luxurious captivity, and Henry ruled both England and Normandy unchallenged. The final union between England and Normandy was therefore a little less than fifty years old, and had depended on the attitudes of the great lords who had estates in both territories. Although they saw themselves as Norman, they quickly came to regard their English lands as at least equal, and sometimes more valuable, than their Norman holdings: we have to remember that by the end of Henry I's reign, there were few English lords or bishops left, and the vast majority of the ruling class were Norman.

The balance of power between the king, his barons and the Church was a problem which was very much at the forefront of politics. The relationship between the ruler and his vassals was to bedevil English politics until the reign of Edward III; and even then this was only a lull in a conflict that continued into the Tudor era. The fates of both Stephen and Matilda, Henry's successors, were determined by their dealings with the great lords: Matilda was too imperious and remote, while Stephen's inability to maintain order proved to be his eventual downfall. At worst, his reign was notoriously a time of anarchy and civil war, vividly depicted by an anonymous Anglo-Saxon writer who regarded this period as a disaster for his people:

> [When the barons] saw that Stephen was a good-humoured, kindly, and easy-going man who inflicted no punishment, then they committed all manner of horrible crimes ... For every great man built himself castles and held them against the king; and they filled the whole land with these castles. They sorely burdened the unhappy people of the country with forced labour on the castles; and when the castles were built, they filled them up with devils and wicked men. By night and by day they seized those whom they believed to have any wealth, whether they were men or women; and in order to get their gold and silver, they put them into prison and tortured them with unspeakable tortures ... And men said openly that Christ and His saints slept.[12]

Henry may have been favoured as Stephen's heir because the magnates thought that the status quo would be maintained if the young prince succeeded to the throne. But Henry was more than their match: working in subtle stages, he always appeared to consult them so that they could not claim that anything had been done without their agreement. They had no agenda other than their own self-interest, which did, however, include a desire for the restoration of some kind of order. Henry played on this, and the barons found that they had underestimated his unequalled – and almost irresistible – powers of persuasion. With their advice and consent as part of the great council of the realm, he had manoeuvred himself into a position where he was in control of the kingdom and had organized matters to his own satisfaction. In 1157, three years after he came to the throne, he felt secure enough to settle matters with two of the most powerful earls, Hugh Bigod of Norfolk and William of Blois, son of King Stephen, by depriving both of them of their castles at a great council at Bury St Edmunds, and putting this sentence into immediate effect. Overall, the settlement of 1154 which returned lands to those who had possessed them at the death of Henry I was a success, evidence of Henry II's carefully considered judgement in such matters. One chronicler called him 'Henry the Peacemaker' for the way in which he handled this potentially explosive situation.

Henry's character was of course formed by his parentage and education. His grandfather was Henry I, 'a master builder: of men, of personal relationships, of institutions',[13] who laid the foundations of the institutions of the English kingdom on which the younger Henry was to build. When the new prince was born, on 5 March 1133, he was generally recognized as the heir to the English throne, though his claim to it was through his mother Matilda, and England had never had a female ruler. The old king, anxious to secure the future of the orderly kingdom he had created, had made the English barons swear an oath of allegiance to Matilda and her son Henry soon after the latter's birth. But when Henry I died in 1135, the succession was disputed by Stephen, Count of Blois and Matilda's cousin, though his claim, too, was doubtful, as he was himself the son of one of William the Conqueror's daughters. The arguments on both sides had never been tested before, and when Matilda and Stephen appealed to the pope for a decision, the case turned on the testimony of Hugh Bigod, Earl of Norfolk, who claimed that Henry I had absolved the barons from their oath to Matilda on his deathbed. But no other witness came forward to support this, and the pope refused to decide between the contestants. Stephen had seized the English throne in the meanwhile, as Matilda was in Anjou with her husband, Geoffrey, Count of Anjou.

The underlying problem was not merely that England had never been ruled by a queen in her own right, but that a female sovereign was unheard of in Western Europe. Heiresses such as Eleanor of Aquitaine might inherit duchies, but kingdoms, and the quasi-sacred office of king, were subject to different conventions. Matilda's personality did not help: she had been married to Henry V, ruler of the Holy Roman Empire, and was therefore known as the Empress Matilda: proud and insensitive, she alienated her subjects even before she had had a chance to make good her claim to the throne. But she was also persistent in adversity: by 1141, her supporters in England were relatively few, after six years of warfare and a series of setbacks for her allies. At the end of that year, she was besieged by Stephen at Oxford Castle: she had no allies who could come to her aid, and instead escaped across the frozen moat in a white cloak, making her way through the enemy lines unnoticed.

Yet two years later, she summoned the young Henry, aged ten, to join her in England, and placed him under the care of his uncle Earl Robert of Gloucester, who held court at Bristol. Robert's court was a meeting place for scholars. William of Malmesbury, perhaps the greatest English historian of the day, was commissioned to write his history of recent events by the earl. Likewise, Geoffrey of Monmouth had dedicated a copy of his great work on Welsh history and on King Arthur, *The History of the Kings of Britain*, to Robert. Other men at Bristol included Adelard of Bath, one of a handful of Christian scholars who were in touch with their Spanish counterparts who translated works from the Arabic. This was the heyday of Arab science and Adelard's treatise *On the Astrolabe*, an instrument used by astronomers and navigators, was dedicated to the young Henry at about this time. Henry was at Bristol for perhaps two years; when he returned to Normandy, his tutor was William of Conches, another scholar with a great reputation who studied Islamic science and also advocated the reading of classical Latin texts. These teachers laid the foundations of Henry's interest in learning. In 1150, he spent time in Anjou at the court of his father Geoffrey, who was also a lover of book learning. There is a story that Geoffrey, during a long and intractable siege of the castle of one of his rebellious vassals, passed the time by reading the standard work on strategy and tactics by the Roman author Vegetius, and he was said to prefer reading to hunting.

But Geoffrey played relatively little part in his son's upbringing; his marriage to Matilda was largely a political manoeuvre, and although three children were born of the match, Matilda spent long periods in England away from her husband, and Henry, as heir to the English throne, was often with her. Henry was with his father for the two years before the latter's death, however, when they campaigned together in Normandy. Geoffrey is described as charming, red-headed and a great warrior: Henry inherited his red hair and his military skill, but less of his evidently superficial charm. Matilda was a much greater influence on her son, partly through their shared experiences in England attempting to make good her claim to the throne, and partly because he trusted her and took her advice. She had learned her skills as Empress of Germany in negotiations on her husband's behalf, and Walter Map ascribes 'all the points in which the king was vexatious' to her teaching. She had taught Henry to prolong the settlement of petitions and lawsuits so that he could keep in his thrall those seeking his favour in such matters, and if posts fell vacant where the revenues during a vacancy went to the crown, to keep them open for as long as possible: 'an unruly hawk, if meat is often offered to it and then snatched away or hid, becomes keener and more obedient'.[14] Map was undoubtedly biased: he goes on to call her 'most evil'. In reality she seems to have been a shrewd and practical adviser; an interview between her and an emissary from Thomas Becket at the height of the quarrel with the king is described in a letter that survives, in which her views are recorded. These differ from those of her son over the freedom of the Church, but acknowledge the problems that he is trying to solve. Henry seems to have consulted her during her long retirement at a priory near Rouen, where she lived from 1148 until her death in 1167. He inherited from her his shrewd judgement and persistence, but not the haughty demeanour which had made her unpopular in England.

Henry was capable of swift and decisive action. This applied not only in warfare, but in other affairs as well. His boldest stroke was his marriage to Eleanor of Aquitaine, when he was only nineteen. Duchess of Aquitaine in her own right, she had been married to Louis VII, by whom she had two daughters. The marriage had not been an easy one – she is said to have exclaimed, 'I have married a monk, not a king',[15] and the pope had to reconcile the couple in 1149. Louis, desperate to have a son and heir, had procured a divorce in 1152. Within nine weeks, she and Henry were married. Eleanor of Aquitaine was an even more formidable character than Matilda. It is perfectly possible that she, some ten years older than Henry, was the instigator of their marriage, and there were rumours of her love for the young and handsome count when she was still married to Louis. She bore Henry eight children between 1153 and 1167: all survived to adulthood, except William, the eldest, who died at the age of two. The couple were often separated by affairs of state, but Eleanor played a considerable part in the administration of both England and Aquitaine for the first twenty years of Henry's reign. Yet, for reasons that are very obscure, she joined the rebellion of Henry's sons in 1173, and as a result spent the next ten years in confinement, though how harsh the conditions were we do not know. After the death of Henry, her second son, in 1183, she was allowed more freedom, but she never enjoyed the

king's full trust again: as he had with Becket, he never forgave Eleanor for her treachery. She had been a genuine
partner in the building of the Plantagenet empire and val-
ued highly her status as Duchess of Aquitaine; it may be
that the trigger for her participation in the rebellion was the
homage* of the Count of Toulouse in 1173 to Henry II
rather than to herself, as the overlordship of Toulouse
belonged to Aquitaine. After Henry's death, Richard I
restored her lands and revenues, and gave her power to act
for him in England when necessary.

Henry and Eleanor's four surviving sons grew up in a very
different world from the harsh school of warfare and politics
in which Henry had been embroiled in his teens. Henry was
said by Gerald of Wales to have lavished on his children
when they were young 'more than a father's affection, but
in their more advanced years he looked askance at them
like a stepfather'.[16] A modern biographer declares that
'Henry II showed a remarkable capacity for deceiving himself about his sons, and an astonishing indulgence even to
their most patent duplicity'.[17] We know little about their
upbringing, except that Henry, his eldest surviving son, was
placed in Becket's household for a year in 1162, and that he
remained fond of Becket to the end of his life. The problem

---

* The ceremony by which a landholder acknowledged that he held
his territory from a particular lord; the king was the ultimate lord,
at the summit of the pyramid of power, but kings could also hold
lands from other kings: Henry was King of England, but vassal of
the King of France for the lands he controlled in France.

which ruined Henry's relationship with the younger Henry, and then with the rest of his sons, was the question of who should wield power. The king had already shown that he would not tolerate power sharing by his direct rule in what were technically Eleanor's lands in Aquitaine. The situation was made much more difficult to control by Henry's decision to crown the young Henry as king, something he had planned since 1162 and which was finally carried out in 1170. This was intended to secure the succession, and may have been a decision influenced by what had happened on the death of Henry I: if the heir was already crowned, there could be no dispute. But the young Henry was impatient, and his irritation was further exacerbated by the fact that by 1173 his three brothers were all granted lands over which they had genuine authority, while the young king was merely his father's shadow in terms of power. He was more at home in the new world of chivalry, with its lavish expenditure on tournaments, minstrels and feasts. Twice Henry settled with his son by offering him money, once in 1174 and again in 1182. The young king was a popular hero, tall, blond, eloquent and generous, more like his grandfather Geoffrey of Anjou than his father. But he was also greedy, frivolous and inconsistent, and had none of his father's skills in politics and warfare: and this may be the reason why Henry so strenuously avoided putting him in a position of responsibility.

Richard was a different matter. He was given Poitou to rule in 1174, with the brief of dealing with its endlessly rebellious barons. He at once demonstrated his ruthlessness and his military expertise, and within three years he had suppressed the rebellion. In the process, he made many enemies, but he loved Aquitaine above all else. After the young king's death in 1183, Richard became heir to England and Normandy, and when Henry proposed to give Aquitaine to John, he was adamant that this should not happen. He might fight the barons of Aquitaine, but he was also steeped in its ways and culture. His grandfather William X of Aquitaine had been a poet, and Richard likewise wrote verse, in the tradition of the troubadours. Chiefly remembered today for their love poetry, the troubadours also wrote about political matters, and it was political verse that Richard seems to have composed.

Geoffrey, the third son, who became Duke of Brittany, was cordially disliked by his contemporaries. Although he governed Brittany well, developing work which his father had begun, he was a disruptive force in the last years of Henry's reign; Gerald of Wales called him 'overflowing with words, smooth as oil, possessed by his syrupy and persuasive eloquence, of the power of dissolving the apparently indissoluble, able to corrupt two kingdoms with his tongue, of tireless endeavour and a hypocrite in everything',[18] while for one of the most sober chroniclers of the time, he was simply 'that son of perdition'.[19] As to John, the youngest, who played relatively little part in the revolt against his father, Henry seems to have treated him as something of a favourite. Gerald of Wales, soon after Henry's death, called John pleasure-seeking, unable to bear criticism and foolish: when he was sent to Ireland in 1185, he failed to pay his troops, gave huge land grants to his own followers, and mocked the clothes and customs of the native Irish. None the less, by 1187 it was rumoured that Henry planned to make John his heir instead of Richard. John remained with Henry until the last days, and then finally abandoned him and went off to Richard just before his father died.

In an age when kings frequently had mistresses, Henry was relatively discreet. It was about the time of Eleanor's imprisonment that his liaison with Rosamund Clifford became public, and two centuries later London chroniclers related the almost certainly fictional story of how Eleanor had Rosamund bled to death in a hot bath at the royal hunting lodge at Woodstock. Henry had rebuilt Woodstock for Rosamund, complete with a garden in the style of those at Norman palaces in Sicily. The irrepressible Gerald of Wales claimed that Henry had long had a secret affair with her, and there is indeed good evidence that they were lovers, such as a deed in which Henry grants a manor to Walter Clifford 'for the love of Rosamund his daughter'.[20] She was buried at Godstow, and Henry endowed the nunnery richly. Otherwise, Henry is known to have had two illegitimate children before he was married, who were openly acknowledged. All the writers who have left pen-portraits of him stress his avoidance of carnal indulgence and carnal pleasure.

This, then, is the man himself, based on the accounts of his contemporaries, which range from the admiring to the downright hostile: let us now turn to his acts and deeds.

# 2

# His Story

In 1147, the fourteen-year-old Henry landed in England in command of his own army. The forces he brought were wholly inadequate to challenge Stephen's established hold on the kingdom, and he was abandoned by his men after a few weeks because he was unable to pay them. Matilda was still in England, but lacked both supporters and money, and left for Normandy in March 1148: she was never to return to the kingdom for which she had fought for a decade, and effectively retired from active politics. Henry held on for a few months, but the death of Earl Robert of Gloucester, his main supporter, made his situation impossible. He could not even afford to escape, as Robert's heir flatly refused to help him. Typically, instead of surrendering, he boldly sent a secret message to Stephen offering to withdraw if the king would send him money; and Stephen took up the offer.

Henry was potentially heir to the kingdom of England and the duchy of Normandy, as well as Geoffrey's counties of Anjou and Maine. In 1147 his chances of inheriting all of these lands seemed slim: England was securely held by King Stephen, and because so many Norman lords also had English lands, there was a danger of losing Normandy, which Geoffrey ruled in Matilda's name. But the reverse was also true: if Henry or his father were in firm control of Normandy, the better for Henry's chances of regaining the English crown.

Henry was now acting on his own as far as England was concerned. His mother had left her supporters in disarray, and his father was not in a position to help him, as he was fully occupied on the continent. Henry's next attempt at invasion, in 1149, had as its principal object a journey to Scotland, because Henry was anxious to be knighted by his great-uncle, King David of Scotland. As potential heir to a kingdom, he needed if possible to be given this honour, which marked his coming of age, by someone of royal rank. This was achieved at Carlisle at Whitsun, at a great feast attended by three of the English earls who supported Henry's cause. The importance of this in propaganda terms is indicated by the fact that Stephen immediately riposted by having his own son and heir, Eustace, knighted.

Henry travelled to the West Country, where his main support lay; despite the death of Earl Robert, other lords in the area favoured Henry's cause. A brief campaign followed, in which Henry scored his first military success, the capture of the town and castle of Bridport; but this was the only notable event in a campaign in which Stephen's forces generally had the upper hand, and early in 1150, Henry decided once again to beat a retreat to the continent. Here, at the age of seventeen, he acquired his first territory: his father, Geoffrey, transferred the government of Normandy to him in a ceremony at Rouen, and Henry adopted the traditional title of 'Duke of the Normans'. He took over his father's team of officials, and began to learn what was to become one of his great skills, the administration of government and law, an area in which Geoffrey himself had been expert. The following year, a long-standing quarrel between Geoffrey and one of his vassals in the south of the county of Anjou developed into a wider war when the vassal invoked the help of Louis VII of France as Geoffrey's overlord. The war which followed ended in August in stalemate, and it was agreed that the dispute should be settled by the arbitration of Bernard of Clairvaux, founder of the Cistercian order, and one of the great political and religious figures of the day.

For this arbitration, Henry and Geoffrey had to go to Paris. Here Henry saw for the first time the splendour of the French court and of the French capital, the intellectual heart of Europe. In the mid twelfth century, the university was starting to take shape as the great teachers of the day began to group themselves in Paris, in an extraordinary ferment of scholarly activity. Henry almost certainly met Eleanor, Duchess of Aquitaine, then wife of Louis VII, for the first time on this visit. The negotiations with Louis involved some hard bargaining. There is some evidence that Geoffrey was reluctant to compromise, and that Henry was anxious to reach an agreement so that he could go to England yet again, since a bad harvest had left the English discontented with Stephen's rule and inclined to look to Henry for good government. In the end, Henry did homage to Louis for Normandy, which he had avoided performing the previous year; in return, some lands on the border of Normandy and France were transferred to Louis.

Henry and Geoffrey were now able to plan together a new invasion of England, and a council was arranged at Lisieux in Normandy on 14 September to discuss this with the Norman barons. It was a hot summer, and as Geoffrey travelled to his headquarters at Le Mans in the county of Maine, he stopped on the way to bathe in a pool in the forest. But the welcoming coolness of the water led to a chill, and he died at a nearby castle on 7 September. He was only thirty-eight. On his deathbed, he was anxious to prevent Henry from seizing the whole inheritance, leaving nothing for his other son and namesake, Geoffrey, and made his barons swear that they would not bury him until Henry had taken an oath, without knowing the precise terms of the settlement, to obey his father's wishes. Henry reluctantly did so, but was pleased to find that the terms were not as onerous as he had feared: he was to have Anjou and Maine until such time as he was recognized as King of England, at which point he was to hand them over to his brother. For the moment, Henry, aged only eighteen, was established as one of the greatest vassals of the French king.

He was soon to be as powerful as the French king himself. If Geoffrey's death had been unexpected, the next development was even more surprising. Relations between Louis VII and his queen had been fraught for some time. This was partly due to Eleanor's failure to provide him with a much-needed son and heir, but also to the difference in their characters. She had insisted on accompanying him on crusade to Palestine in 1147, much to the scandal of orthodox crusaders. While in the East, she developed a close relationship with her uncle, the Prince of Antioch, both politically and personally, and rumours were rife. On their way back from the East, matters between Louis and Eleanor had grown so bad that the pope himself tried to reconcile them when they met him near Rome in October 1149. The question of a separation arose, and possibly a divorce. The rules about marrying relatives were cast so broadly by the Church at this period that it was possible to draw up a family tree to show that almost any noble married couple were related 'within the prohibited degrees', and their marriages could therefore be annulled on grounds of husband and wife being too closely related. This was true of Louis and Eleanor, and was the official reason for the divorce when Louis decided to act, early in 1152. The king went to Aquitaine and demolished the fortifications he had built there and withdrew the French officials who were running the duchy on his behalf, returning it to Eleanor. On 21 March, a council of the French clergy met and dissolved the marriage. Eleanor and her entourage left Paris for Blois, on their way to the capital of the duchy of Aquitaine at Poitiers.

It proved a most hazardous journey, because Eleanor was now the greatest prize in France for ambitious unmarried noblemen. Louis had failed to make any special provision for retaining control over whom she might marry, relying simply on such control as he had as her feudal lord. The need for such permission for a vassal's marriage, as he knew perfectly well, was often disregarded. The first to try his hand was Count Theobald of Blois, and Eleanor had to make a hurried exit to Tours. Here she was almost ambushed by Henry's younger brother Geoffrey, but left the town by an unexpected route. She also had to avoid the three castles that belonged to him which lay on the road south, before she reached Poitiers and the safety of her own domains.

Yet there would be no real safety until she had found a husband who could ensure that her authority as duchess was maintained. The barons of Aquitaine were notoriously independent, and while her status would be respected, practical government without strong support would be difficult. Eleanor needed to make the right political match, and one candidate stood out from all others, a match that would also mean that Louis was faced with an alliance which had greater power in his kingdom than the king himself. How exactly matters were arranged between Eleanor and Henry, Duke of Normandy and Count of Anjou and Maine, we do not know. Henry had summoned a council at Lisieux on 6 April to discuss military matters, almost certainly another invasion of England: instead, the council was asked to approve his marriage plans, and on 18 May at Poitiers the marriage of Eleanor and Henry was celebrated. The great east window of the cathedral commemorates their union, a glory of red and blue Romanesque glass, in which, at the foot of the crucifixion, they and their children are shown as the donors of this masterpiece.

Eleanor was twenty-nine and Henry nineteen. Together, they ruled an empire which now stretched from the Channel to the Pyrenees, with claims over the county of Toulouse that took their potential domains down to the Mediterranean. Eleanor was a fitting match for the dynamic Henry: one of the greatest beauties of the age, celebrated for her patronage of poets and chroniclers. An early version in French of the Arthurian legend, *The Romance of Brutus*, was dedicated to her, as well as a sequel on the ancestors of the dukes of Normandy. It was through her that the links between the poetry of the troubadours, written in Provençal, and the poetry of the north of France, written in French, came about, and it was at her daughter Marie's court in Champagne that the first romances about Arthur's knights were composed. She herself lived on in the verses of the German followers of the troubadours, as an exemplar of the most desirable of women:

> If the whole world were mine
> From the sea's edge to the Rhine,
> I'd gladly lose it all
> If the queen of England
> Was lying in my arms.[1]

Henry had brought off a major coup: but he must have expected the consequences. He was about to embark for England when news came that Louis had allied himself with the disappointed suitors, Geoffrey and Theobald of Blois, and had invaded Normandy. Henry took the army he had gathered for the invasion of England south to confront the French. His prompt action forced Louis to retreat; he then dealt with his brother's supporters and captured Geoffrey himself. Shortly after this, Louis fell ill and was obliged to seek a truce. By the end of 1152, Henry was ready to return to his English plans.

On 6 January 1153, the feast of Epiphany, a small squadron of ships appeared off the Dorset coast. Their exact landfall is unknown, but could well have been Weymouth or Poole

Harbour. From them, Henry disembarked with a fighting force of perhaps fifteen hundred men. He had come to make good his claim to the English throne, by rallying his friends in England against the man who, in his view, had usurped his rights, Stephen of Blois. A later story tells how immediately after he landed, he went to a nearby chapel, and that as he entered, the priest was intoning the opening words of the lesson for Epiphany, 'Behold the Lord our governor and the kingdom in His hand', as favourable an omen as he could have hoped for.

It seemed impossible that a man of twenty with such a small force could hope to overthrow a well-established ruler who had had possession of England for most of the previous eighteen years. But Henry had both considerable experience of warfare and a continuing power base in the West Country, where his chief remaining supporters in England were based, at Bristol and Gloucester. Stephen's stronghold in the area was at Malmesbury, and Henry attacked this, but failed to take the castle within the town. However, Stephen himself, who had been a popular figure at the beginning of his reign, had earned the distrust of the great lords by his arbitrary arrests of men such as Geoffrey de Mandeville, Earl of Essex, and the barons who did support him were engaged in continual fighting among themselves. Stephen tried to relieve Malmesbury, but had to agree a truce, under which the castle was to be demolished. However, in a move which augured ill for Stephen's cause, the knight sent to supervise the demolition decided to change sides, and instead handed over the castle to Henry intact.

Henry's main problem was that Stephen exercised control over much of England from a series of well-fortified castles. Besieging a fortress was difficult, with the primitive machinery of the time. Henry could try to persuade lords to change allegiance, as in the case of the Earl of Leicester, whose thirty castles in the Midlands were obtained in return for a new charter of rights in Henry's name. Others, such as the castle belonging to the Earl of Derby at Tutbury, had to be besieged: but when it was taken, the earl decided to join what he believed to be the winning side. Here and at Stamford, taken soon afterwards, siegecraft proved to be a vital skill.

Henry now moved to try to raise Stephen's siege of Wallingford. Controlled by Henry's supporters, the castle commanded the vital route along the Thames valley. Raids and counter-raids continued into October, until it seemed that a pitched battle was inevitable. Neither side, however, was prepared to take the risk, and by the end of the month a truce was agreed. Full negotiations began at Winchester on 6 November, but Henry now held the trump card. During the summer, Eustace, Stephen's son and heir, had died during a campaign against Henry's supporters in East Anglia. Henry was now the main contender for his grandfather's inheritance after Stephen's death, regardless of the status of Stephen's own claim to the throne. So an agreement was rapidly reached by which Stephen was to be king for the rest of his life, and Henry did homage to him accordingly. On his death, the succession would pass to Henry and his heirs. Once this agreement was in place, it remained to restore law and order, reaffirm earlier laws and provide for the demolition of the many castles built without the king's licence as bases for plundering the countryside. Estates which had been wrongfully acquired were to be restored, and the mercenaries employed by both sides were to be sent back to the continent. All this was settled in theory, and the agreement was signed by the end of that month.

Theoretical co-operation in restoring peace was one thing, practice another: there were still two administrations in the country, the condemned castles had to be physically demolished, and each side had its own agenda in terms of making sure its supporters were kept happy. There were the inevitable disputes, and progress was slow; but nevertheless Henry was sufficiently sure that the agreement would work to decide to return to Normandy in April 1154, where he negotiated a peace with Louis VII in the summer. In late October, he received unexpected news: King Stephen had died of a chill at Faversham in Kent, and Theobald, the Archbishop of Canterbury, was acting as regent. As a chronicler of the time commented: 'although England was without a king for almost six weeks ... the peace was not disturbed by God's grace, either for love or fear of the new ruler'.[2] It was to be twenty years before England's peace was troubled again.

Henry reached England on 8 December 1154, with Eleanor and his brother Geoffrey, and presumably his baby son, William. Theobald crowned Henry in London on 19 December, after he had been acclaimed as king according to the ancient English ritual. To his existing titles, Duke of Normandy and Aquitaine, Count of Anjou and Maine, Henry could add that of King of England, and less formally, that of being the greatest ruler in the Western world. He was still only twenty-one.

Henry's first task was to rebuild the institutions that had been weakened during the anarchy of the civil wars, and to reinstate royal control over the barons in England who were loath to give up their new-found independence. Immediately after his coronation, he issued the customary charter expected of a new king. Rather than confirming the grants made by his immediate predecessors, as would have been usual, Henry instead decreed a return to the status quo under his grandfather. This immediately challenged all the lords who had benefited from the anarchy to acquire lands belonging to the king or Church. And in the New Year of 1155 he began a systematic campaign to enforce the agreed destruction of the unlicensed castles which had been built in the years of strife: Stephen had made little headway with this. More dramatically, Henry abolished all the earldoms granted by Stephen to his followers, and took back the royal lands that had supported them. Henry's customary luck also helped: two extensive estates in the Midlands came into his hands, both held by Ranulph, Earl of Chester. Prior to Ranulph's death, it was alleged that William Peverel, lord of the honour of Peverel in the Peak, had poisoned him. Henry had granted Ranulph William's lands unless William could clear himself in court of the charges brought against him; William had fled, and was not heard of again. This enabled the king to begin another urgent task, the restoration of the royal finances, as the royal treasury had been almost completely exhausted by Stephen.

By 1157, there were only 217 baronial castles against 52 royal ones: a quarter of all castles thus belonged to the king. It was said that over a thousand had been destroyed, and there was no question about the huge shift in the balance of power away from the great lords. The actual confiscation of baronial estates was mitigated by Henry making grants of the same lands back to their owners. The effect of this was to ensure that the barons recognized his authority; and even charters he himself had issued during the anarchy were replaced by new grants. There was little resistance in England to these measures; the lords, like the common people, were weary of the endless skirmishes and uncertainties of civil war.

Henry had not quite yet lost his appetite for extending his empire, however. He laid plans for an invasion of Ireland, which was to become a fief for his youngest brother, William, and obtained papal blessing for the expedition. The idea was mooted at a council of the great lords in September, but came to nothing, partly because of the opposition of Henry's mother, Matilda, whose opinions Henry respected. His other brother, Geoffrey, was more of a problem. Under the terms of the oath that Henry had had to swear before inheriting Anjou and Maine, these two counties were to go to Geoffrey should Henry regain England. Henry was reluctant to give them up, and once again luck came to his rescue: later that year, the duchy of Brittany was offered to Geoffrey by the inhabitants, who had ejected their duke, and Geoffrey accepted. Not only was the potential for rebellion removed, because Geoffrey now had sufficient lands of his own, but also there was now a friendly ruler on the western border of Normandy and Maine.

On Henry's next visit to England in April 1157, he turned his attention to the countries on the English borders. He had long wanted to consolidate the English foothold in Wales, and that summer he launched an offensive against Owain, King of Gwynedd in north Wales. It was a large and well-organized force, and Owain was attacked from both land and sea. But it nearly ended in disaster when the Welsh ambushed Henry while his army was marching in two separate divisions. His troops were thrown into confusion, and the standard-bearer, Henry of Essex, dropped the royal ensign, leading the rest of the army to believe that King Henry himself had been killed. It was only with the arrival of the other half of the army that the attackers were driven off. Henry made peace with Owain, and recovered some of the lands lost to the Welsh during Stephen's reign. Rhys ap Griffith, ruler of Deheubarth in south Wales, had also refused to acknowledge Henry's authority, but now volunteered his submission. About the same time, he was also able to negotiate the return of counties which Stephen had lost to the Scottish king.

When Henry crossed the Channel to Anjou in August 1158, he did not return for more than four years. His first great objective was to recover three key castles on the Norman border from Louis VII that had been given to him for recognizing Henry's father as duke. Henry therefore proposed that his eldest surviving son, Henry, should be betrothed to Louis's daughter Margaret, and the three castles in question should be her dowry. This meant diplomatic negotiations at the highest level, and he sent his chancellor Thomas Becket, his most trusted adviser, who had been in his service since shortly after his coronation. It was on this occasion that Becket set out with a magnificent display of wealth which only served to heighten the effect of Henry's own modest entourage. The mission duly succeeded and the betrothal was arranged: the castles were placed in the guardianship of the Knights Templar until the couple were married.

Henry now set out to try to enforce Eleanor's rights as Duchess of Aquitaine to the overlordship of the county of Toulouse, which would have extended his empire to the Mediterranean. Becket was again at the king's right hand during this ambitious – perhaps overambitious – expedition. A very considerable army was assembled at Poitiers at midsummer in 1159, despite the danger that Louis himself might join the opponents of Henry's claim: Louis's sister was married to Raymond, Count of Toulouse, who denied that he was a vassal of Aquitaine. Not only had Henry sworn an oath of loyalty to Louis, but the person of the French king as ultimate lord of these lands was particularly sacred. If Louis was on the battlefield, Henry would have the unwelcome dilemma of either breaking his feudal oath by attacking Louis, or simply withdrawing and leaving the field to the French king and his allies.

Henry brought over a small number of knights from England, a contingent of Scottish knights led by Malcolm, the eighteen-year-old King of Scotland, and a group of Welsh foot soldiers. In addition there were levies from

Aquitaine, troops raised by the Count of Barcelona and a horde of mercenaries. Becket was deputed to capture as many of Raymond's personal domains as he could, thus depriving him of money and other resources, while Henry moved to besiege Toulouse. He moved swiftly, indeed too swiftly: his nearest supply base was forty miles from the city. When he arrived, however, Louis was unexpectedly already within the city; an epidemic broke out in the besiegers' camp, and Henry judged it prudent to withdraw. Becket was deputed to cover the retreat and, 'donning hauberk and helmet',[3] captured three important castles. At the end of the year, a truce was agreed, to last until Whitsun 1160. When it expired, neither side were in the mood for further fighting, and peace was made. It was not particularly favourable to Henry: all captured castles, with a few exceptions in the south, were to be returned, and the Count of Evreux, who had gone over to Henry's side, was to return to his old allegiance. This was effectively the end of Henry's attempts to maximize his territory in France.

In the summer of 1160, Constance, Louis's queen, died, and Louis married again very shortly afterwards. This meant that the marriage treaty negotiated by Becket's splendid embassy in 1158 might well become valueless, as Louis might have further children, and would be reluctant to let Margaret have more than a small portion of his domains, particularly if he had an heir. Henry decided to strike while the going was good, and ensure the surrender of the three castles due on her marriage. As papal legates were conveniently in Normandy at the time, he asked them for permission for young Henry and Margaret to be married, despite being infants aged five and two respectively. The papal legates agreed, and performed the ceremony on 2 November. The Knights Templar duly handed over the castles; the irregularity of the whole procedure was confirmed by the large gifts that Henry made to the order for their assistance.

Although the king had been absent from England for three years, he seemed in no hurry to return, and spent a further year in Normandy, largely concerning himself with administrative matters, before he crossed the Channel, landing at Southampton on 25 January 1163. Here he would find himself involved in a new and very different struggle. Henry's territorial power in France had brought him into conflict with Louis VII; in England, possibly the most advanced state in Western Europe in terms of royal administration, his royal authority brought him into conflict with the Church. The Archbishop of Canterbury, Theobald, had played a crucial part in bringing Henry to the English throne by refusing to crown Stephen's son Eustace, and had always worked to preserve the unity of the kingdom and its place in the Anglo-Norman empire. He had gathered round him a household which was a centre of learning, and which was to provide both the Church and state with a series of great bishops and administrators, as well as including some of the leading scholars of Europe. Theobald was concerned to maintain an amicable relationship with the king and to further his interests where possible.

On Theobald's death in April 1161, Henry evidently decided to try to forge even closer links by arranging for the election of Thomas Becket as archbishop. He seems to have believed that his chancellor would owe his chief loyalty to the state, and would share his aims. But before entering the king's service Becket had been a member of Theobald's household, even though he was not in holy orders, and Henry may have underestimated the influence of this early experience. On the one hand, his education there – for the household was a kind of learned academy, backed up by the great library at Canterbury – had fitted him for the office of chancellor; on the other, there was perhaps a deeper, hidden attachment to the Church that Becket's dazzling display of secular splendour and urbane manner had concealed from the king. In May 1162, Becket was elected archbishop, as Henry wished: the king had sent his justiciar, Richard de Lucy, to England, and said to him before he went, 'If I were lying dead on my bier, would you do everything in your power to put my son Henry on the throne?' De Lucy answered, 'All I could.' Henry continued: 'I want you to do as much to get the chancellor elected to the see of Canterbury.'[4] Becket himself seems to have had serious doubts about the appointment, perhaps realizing that his own personal devotion to the Church was far stronger than Henry appreciated. When the king raised the subject privately with him, Becket answered by pointing to his rich clothes and saying ironically, 'How religious, how saintly is the man you would appoint to that holy see!'[5]

The process of election itself lay on the fault line between the opposing claims of Church and state. The English kings saw the archbishop and other prelates as great magnates, holding wide lands for which they were responsible to the king, providing troops for his armies and revenues for the

Exchequer. Because such resources were vital to the royal government, it was essential for the king to have his input in the election of Church leaders. The Church, however, saw them as purely spiritual clerics, in whose appointment the state should not interfere. Pope Gregory VII's pronouncement on this in 1075 had led to the 'Investiture Contest' in Germany, which became a direct and personal conflict between Gregory and Henry IV, the Holy Roman Emperor. In the Anglo-Norman realm, a complicated compromise had been worked out in 1107, that the future prelate should do homage to the king before his consecration to spiritual office, and the elections were to be made by the relevant authority within the Church: in the case of Canterbury, this authority lay with the abbot and monks of St Augustine's. The election, however, was to be made in a royal court and under the supervision of the king's official.

Although this remained the procedure long after Henry's time, the Church had moved on dramatically between 1107 and 1162. There had been a sea change in religious attitudes, reflected by the rise of the new religious orders, notably the Cistercians. Spiritual ideals came to the fore, and throughout the Church there was a growing belief that such ideals should not be tainted by secular considerations. Cistercian abbots were often appointed as bishops, and in the international chapters of the Cistercian order, the latest concepts of the Church's role were freely discussed. The pope, not the king, was their superior. Furthermore, the Church as a whole was becoming more organized and was flexing its muscles against the incursions of lay powers. The laws which ruled the Church – canon law as opposed to civil law – were being gradually codified from a mass of ancient and often very local sources into a systematic whole. Around 1140, an Italian lawyer, Gratian, success-fully brought canon law into order in his *Decretum*, which became the standard work on the subject. The Church claimed wide jurisdiction not only over ecclesiastical mat-ters, but also over many aspects of life in which clerics were involved. The most critical of these was the question of which system of justice applied to members of the Church who had been ordained. The Church claimed that they could only be tried in Church courts, and even if convicted of serious crimes such as rape or murder, they could not then be handed over to the secular authority, because they had already been punished – usually by being deprived of their holy orders, the principle being that God did not per-mit a second punishment for the same offence. To plead 'benefit of clergy' was to claim exemption from all secular authority.

Henry may have hoped to resolve this conflict, and to bring about the full restoration of the crown's authority to enforce law and order, by making Becket both chancellor and archbishop. If so, he was almost instantly disappointed. Becket's election as archbishop was made in May 1162, supervised by de Lucy. One bishop, Gilbert Foliot of Here-ford, opposed it: a complex figure, he was ascetic and known for his pious life, but also may have wanted the archbishop-ric for himself. A charitable interpretation is probably that he judged Becket unsuitable because of his outward show, and also because he was not even in holy orders. In a highly unusual – but not unheard of – procedure, Thomas became a priest on 2 June, and on 3 June he was consecrated archbishop. Almost at once, he wrote to the king resigning all his secular offices. Henry's plan had failed at the first hurdle. Curiously, it was Henry of Blois, Bishop of Winchester and brother of King Stephen, who is said to have advised Becket to resign his secular offices, and it was he who arranged that the seven-year-old Prince Henry, Henry's eldest son, acting for his father, should release him from his lay obligations. Becket was later said to have warned Henry that his appointment would be fatal to their relationship. Becket was ambitious, but also very focused: he had not expected to become archbishop, and when he did, he may even have surprised himself with his reaction to the new situation. We come back to the idea that his early training as a cleric had only been overlaid by the trappings of secular power, and that he realized on becoming archbishop an underlying spiritual vocation which had until now been suppressed. 'He threw off the layman and became the complete archbishop.'[6]

Prince Henry went to meet his father when he landed at Southampton in January 1163. He was accompanied by Becket, who had been appointed as his tutor the previous year. The king was equally overjoyed to see both of them, and it looked as though the old cordiality with his friend would resume. He and Becket talked together at the royal lodging, until Becket, sensing that Henry was tired from the journey, took his leave; and the next day they rode together to London. In March, Henry summoned a great council at

Westminster, and set out his plans for the work that needed to be done in England after his long absence.

The task of repairing the damage done to the king's rights during Stephen's reign was still far from complete, and two great inquiries put in hand at the council were concerned with discovering the true condition of the feudal estates and of the nation's finances. The survey of estates aimed to discover the number of knights who held land on each baron's estate, which was the basis of feudal taxation, and to bring the records up to date.

Becket, as skilled an administrator as Henry, was at about the same time carrying out a survey of the property of Canterbury. Much of it had been seized by local lords in Stephen's reign, and there were still important castles which had not been given back. He had recently returned from a great Church council at Tours, at which edicts against those who took property from the Church had been proclaimed; and he now demanded the restitution of four castles in Kent from their occupiers, without raising the issue with the king. This displeased Henry, and Becket made matters worse by excommunicating one of Henry's tenants-in-chief, who held his land directly from the king, over the right to appoint a vicar to the church at Eynsford. This was in breach of an agreement going back to the days of William the Conqueror, by which no tenant-in-chief could be excommunicated without the king's permission, since such a sentence might hinder them in carrying out their royal duties. It was the first sign of the deep rift, barely a year after Becket's consecration, between the king's views and those of Becket as newly self-appointed champion of the

Church's rights. In the latter's view, the Church's rights as spiritual overlord of the kingdom overruled all royal intervention, and he, as leader of the Church, did not have to consult the king on such matters.

Becket's attitude went further than this: he also saw himself as the champion against any royal attempt to alter established customs, even if these were purely secular. At a council at Woodstock in July 1163, Henry proposed that money formerly paid by taxpayers direct to the sheriffs, who ran the individual counties, to cover the costs of local government and defence, should be paid direct to the Exchequer, which would then reimburse the sheriffs and would be able to oversee their use of the money. Becket called this an arbitrary innovation, and refused to pay anything from the Canterbury estates. It was exactly the kind of scheme which as chancellor he would have implemented; and it seems as if he was determined to set himself up as an antagonist to the king's ambitions to build a strong government. However, his fellow prelates were by no means all supportive of him. Henry had obtained the see of London for Gilbert Foliot, who had opposed Becket's election, and when Foliot was installed as bishop, he refused to renew his oath of allegiance to the archbishop.

If Becket had so far been on doubtful ground, attempting to resist royal demands in matters beyond the immediate reach of canon law, the next source of dissension was much more serious and could be represented as a defence of an ancient right of the Church. Here it was Henry, in his quest for good government, who was testing the limits of his power against what was undoubtedly an innovation on the part of the Church. Canon law was something that had developed rapidly since the death of Henry I, and had gained the support of not only most of the English bishops, particularly those who had trained in Archbishop Theobald's household, but also of the more educated laymen. The ecclesiastical courts were seen as rational and coherent, with procedures which were evidently designed to be fair. Even the fact that serious crimes committed by clerics in major orders (that is, those who had been ordained) might be referred to the pope himself, and thus to an authority outside England, did not seem to be a cause for concern. It was with cases at a humbler level – grave crimes committed by individual clerics in minor orders – that Henry took issue. The royal justices knew of a hundred or more serious cases since 1154 in which clerics had avoided secular justice, and it was notorious that in Stephen's reign pleas of 'benefit of clergy' had been badly misused. Against the Church's argument that God did not permit the same crime to be judged twice, Henry quoted a different section of canon law concerning minor clerics convicted of secular crimes in the Church courts – 'Let them be handed over to the secular court' – which he interpreted as being an injunction to surrender such men, once deprived of their orders, to the royal justices for punishment. The problem was that it was often difficult to establish whether a man was in minor orders or not – it was not just priests who were exempted, but lesser ranks such as deacons. And the so-called 'criminous clerks' often brandished their impunity, as in the case of Philip de Brois. Accused of homicide at the Bishop of Lincoln's court, he secured a rather dubious acquittal. The Sheriff of Bedford claimed that he was not a cleric, and tried to reopen the case. De Brois abused him publicly in open court, which constituted lese-majesty, for which the king managed with difficulty to secure a sentence of a year's exile, but only in the ecclesiastical court itself.

In short, Becket argued that the canon law principle that 'God judges no man twice in the same matter' implied that God did not punish the same crime twice. Henry carefully proposed that the only judgement should be in the ecclesiastical courts, but insisted that once the judgement was made, and the offender deprived of clerical status, he should be handed over to the secular power for the appropriate secular punishment. There was no question of a second trial. Henry's argument was similarly flawed: the phrase he quoted was in the context of establishing the accused's right to clerical status. Once it had been proven that he was indeed a cleric, he was to be handed back to the ecclesiastical court. It was not a question of handing the offender back to the secular court after the sentence according to canon law had been carried out.

Elsewhere in Europe, the issue of criminous clerks never became a major cause of dispute between Church and state; and it only became a major issue in England because of the personalities involved. This was a quarrel between Becket and Henry, as vicious as any quarrel between erstwhile bosom friends could be. Their very different approaches came into the open at the council held at Westminster on 14 October 1163. This had been summoned to adjudicate on a long-standing quarrel as to whether the Archbishop of York owed obedience to the Archbishop of Canterbury as primate of all England. But Henry chose to use his opening speech to set out his desire to bring the criminous clerks to justice, arguing that losing holy orders was not a sufficient deterrent against clerics who might commit such crimes, and indeed insisting that clerics deserved a greater punishment precisely because of their betrayal of their moral authority. Becket replied by rehearsing the precedents for clerical immunity, and depicting the king's proposals as an innovation. Innovation, to the minds of medieval men, was pernicious, an offence against the established order of society as ordained by God, and this was a powerful argument. His fellow bishops supported him against the king; most of them had been appointed since canon law had begun to be highly influential on the thinking of clergy.

Henry's next tactic was to demand that the prelates swear to observe the royal customs. This was a piece of legal chicanery, presenting a choice between an oath which implied they would accept the king's proposals, and a refusal which would be so broad in its effect as to hint at treason. Becket was not to be outdone, however, and answered with another quibble. On the analogy of the oath of fealty which they swore to the king on taking up office, to obey him 'in life and limb and earthly honour saving their order', they would swear to observe the royal customs 'saving their order': in other words, if their duties to the king conflicted with the laws of the Church, they would follow the latter. At this Henry, baulked of his prey, retired in a royal rage.

This meeting set the pattern for the years that followed. Henry, set on securing justice for everyone on an equal footing, was in effect an innovator; Becket, although he would not have admitted it, was also an innovator in terms of the extent of the application of canon law which he proposed. Ultimately it is the personalities that count in such a deadlock. Henry's strength lay in his determination, his weakness in feeling he had been betrayed by Becket and in his susceptibility to violent anger, which was a serious problem in moments of crisis.

Becket, on the other hand, seems to have acted with cool deliberation, verging on a calculating and steely determination to inflict as much damage as he could on the king. He was ready to unleash excommunications, his principal weapon, without the least warning, and without any attempt at negotiation. His inflexible refusal to compromise could be seen as his weakness. Thus it was that soon after Becket became archbishop, relations between the two men broke down irretrievably.

The end of the council of Westminster was a foretaste of what was to come. The proceedings only lasted a day, and the king's closing action was to demand the formal surrender of the castles which had been entrusted to Becket when he was chancellor. He then departed without warning to the city of London. He did make another attempt to come to terms with Becket in late October. The meeting took place at Northampton, outside the town, since there was no room for both the king's court and the archbishop's retinue within the town walls, which implies that Becket was travelling with a substantial entourage. Henry reproached Becket with ingratitude, but an appeal to old friendship fell on deaf ears: Becket was now wholly devoted to the Church, and in reply repeated his offer to take the king's oath with the proviso of 'saving his order' added. He argued that the Church's laws were divine, and if they conflicted with secular laws he could not defy them by obeying Henry.

In the face of such intransigence, Henry gave up any direct approach to Becket, and negotiated with the other bishops. Towards the end of 1163, he persuaded the Archbishop of York and the Bishop of London to swear to obey the royal customs; in exchange, he promised that he would demand nothing from them that was contrary to the privileges of their status as clerics. This at least gave Henry some room for manoeuvre, and he had soon persuaded other bishops to take the same oath.

By this time the pope was aware of the rift between Henry and Becket. Alexander III was one of two popes elected during a political schism in the Church, caused by the rivalry of William I of Sicily and Frederick Barbarossa, the Holy Roman Emperor. On the death of Adrian IV (the only Englishman ever to have become pope) in 1160, the cardinals who supported William – a large majority – elected Alexander III; Barbarossa's supporters elected Victor IV. As the election was supposed to be unanimous, neither pope was entirely legitimate, and both sought the support of the monarchs of Western Christendom. Most of Europe acknowledged Alexander III, but any monarch dissatisfied with Alexander's judgements was liable to defect to the other side, and hence Alexander was very anxious to ensure that Henry continued to support him.

In the late autumn of 1163, Becket received letters from Alexander urging him to comply with Henry's wishes. The archbishop knew exactly what the political position was, and even if it went against his conscience, seems to have been prepared to accept the pope's instructions. He sought out the king at Woodstock, and offered his unconditional submission to Henry's customs. Henry accepted this, but asked that since Becket's refusal had been in public, his acceptance should also be in public, and a great council was summoned at Clarendon, near Oxford, for 25 January 1164. Becket was beginning to have doubts, and it was a day or two before he could be persuaded by Henry's supporters to perform the ceremony. He duly made the submission, and it seemed that the quarrel between the two men was settled.

At this point Henry, desperate to begin work on his plans for the overhaul of the government of England, overplayed his hand. The 'ancient customs' were nowhere actually recorded, but were a matter of tradition, memory and the sworn evidence of suitable witnesses who remembered the usages of the past. Henry, like most twelfth-century rulers, wanted to replace this with a written version of these customs – in effect, a law code. He had therefore prepared a document, drawn up by those of his barons old enough to remember his grandfather's reign, which set out the customs in writing, copied in duplicate on a single sheet of parchment. When the parchment was torn, half the document was handed to each of the two parties concerned; this legal form was called a chirograph, and as proof that the copies were genuine, the torn edges would match when produced as evidence.

Becket saw that his worst fears had been realized. Just as the Church had recently produced an authoritative version of its own laws, Henry was set on doing the same for secular legislation. There would be no room for manoeuvre if he accepted this document, and in any case he believed that Henry had introduced, if not new clauses, at least interpretations of the customs favourable to the royal government. He called the written customs 'pernicious innovations',[7] contrary to canon law, and refused to assent to them. Becket and Henry may both seem incredibly obstinate to us today, but this was a battle with a huge amount at stake for the losing side. A long struggle followed, with the rest of the assembly trying to secure Becket's signature to the document, but the archbishop would only assent verbally to what became known as the Constitutions of Clarendon. The final version records that these 'customs and privileges of the Crown' were 'confirmed by the archbishops, bishops, earls, barons, nobles and elders of the realm',[8] which was, up to a point, true. Henry might have got what he wanted, yet he had forfeited any remaining trust that Becket might have had in him.

Becket's first reaction was to seek the pope's absolution from the oath he had sworn at Clarendon; but Alexander was all too aware that this would constitute open defiance of the king, and might lead to loss of his support – he could not afford to have Henry switch to Victor IV's party. He refused Becket's request. Henry also refused to see Becket: when the latter attempted to meet the king, the park gates at Woodstock were shut in his face. In despair, Becket made two attempts to flee the country: the first time the winds were against him, and on the second occasion the sailors recognized the archbishop and refused to take him for fear of the king. At a subsequent meeting, Henry jestingly referred to this escape attempt, asking if the country was too small to hold them both, but otherwise received him coldly.

Becket had made many enemies at court by his behaviour, and they were now the king's chief advisers. Henry was looking for an opportunity to humiliate the archbishop, with a cold determination that matched Becket's own. He chose a trivial matter. One of Becket's vassals, a certain John the Marshal from Kent, had a case before the archbishop's court. Among the customs recorded by Henry, or more probably written on his instructions, was a clause allowing a vassal who failed to obtain justice in the court of his immediate lord to have the case transferred to the royal court. With tacit royal support, John the Marshal swore in front of two witnesses that Becket had not given him justice, and Becket was cited before the king's court to answer the case. He was too ill to appear when the case came up, and the two knights whom he sent instead to make his excuses were ignored. Henry claimed that the archbishop was holding his court in contempt – which seems to have been entirely unjust – and summoned a great council at Northampton, on 6 October 1164, for the purpose of arraigning Becket for this offence.

The humbling of the archbishop was to be carried out in front of a great assembly, the like of which for splendour men could not remember since the king's coronation ten years earlier. To add to the insult, all those present were summoned by the king's personal writ, with the exception of Becket, who was served with a writ from the Sheriff of Kent – perhaps correct in a strictly legal sense, but yet another indication of Henry's unyielding pursuit of him. And to avoid any contact with Becket before the council, the king arrived late on the night before it was to open, having lingered on the journey by hawking at every opportunity on the way.

Henry listened to Becket's case the next morning, in which Becket repeated the evidence of his knights, accusing John the Marshal of falsehood in swearing on a service book instead of a bible. He also complained of the lack of a personal summons, and pointed out that his adversary was absent. Henry coolly replied that John was away on official duties but would be there tomorrow, and adjourned the court.

The following day, Henry engineered the crisis that he now sought. The accusation of contempt of court was now made formally, and despite Becket's protests that he had the right to judge John, who had made a false oath, the archbishop was convicted. Furthermore, because Becket had sworn to obey the king at his consecration, the court held that he should be sentenced to forfeit all the lands he held from the king and all his goods, and to be at the king's mercy. Henry of Blois, the senior bishop who had persuaded Becket to accept the archbishopric only two years earlier, pronounced the sentence when no one else would do so. To this Becket defiantly replied: 'Even if I were to remain silent at such a sentence, future ages will not.'[9] Henry's desire for revenge on Becket had indeed led him into a travesty of the justice he held in such high esteem.

Becket made his submission, at the desperate pleas of his fellow bishops, but had he known what Henry had in store for him the next day, he very probably would have refused. For Henry now brought up the question of the unsettled debts he had left when he resigned as chancellor. Traditionally, such debts were paid over a period of time to the Exchequer, as the final accounts under each heading were drawn up and agreed. Henry started with a single item, expenditure on two castles; Becket replied that this had also included work on the Tower of London, for which he was responsible at the time, but Henry claimed that the latter work had been done without his authority, and forced Becket to agree to pay the full amount. This he reluctantly did, and several barons supported the archbishop by standing surety for him.

Henry had not finished yet: by the end of the day, he had produced a list of items adding up to £20,000. Becket could not possibly raise this sum, and riposted that he had no notice of these matters before he came to Northampton. It was clear that Henry was moving in for the kill, and the court adjourned on the Friday for the weekend. Frantic discussions followed among Becket's household and the bishops. Suggestions were put forward that ranged from a firm resistance based on the formal quittance which Becket had received when he was consecrated, which absolved him from all secular obligations, to resignation and submission to the king's mercy. By the Sunday, Becket was ill with a fever, and excused himself from attending the court on Monday. Henry simply regarded this as an excuse, and insisted that he appear on the Tuesday.

Becket had evidently decided on outright defiance. He celebrated Mass early that morning, but chose an altar dedicated to St Stephen and used the liturgy for St Stephen's Day, part of which began 'Princes sat and spoke against me'. Some of the king's court were in attendance and at once told the king of Becket's actions, a foretaste of what might be expected in court. When Becket appeared, he took his archbishop's cross from the man who bore it in front of him and brandished it as he strode into the chamber. The proceedings opened with the bishops reporting to the king that Becket had berated them for their judgement against him, reminding them that if the case had been heard in a court in Kent – as it should have been – the fine for his offence would have been forty shillings. He had appealed to the pope, and had forbidden the bishops to judge him on any of the matters of which Henry accused him that had occurred during his chancellorship. Becket himself then spoke, affirming what he had said, and quoting the quittance from secular obligations. The bishops then asked the king to release them from their duty to join the secular court to pass judgement, and Henry reluctantly agreed. Becket and the bishops withdrew, while the lay lords debated the verdict.

What that verdict was we shall never know. When the doors were opened again, the earls appeared to deliver it, but there was a moment of confusion and argument as to who should read it out. Becket took advantage of this to repeat that the proceedings were out of order, that in the case for which he had been summoned, his opponent, John the Marshal, had not appeared, and therefore no sentence could be passed. He ended: 'Such as I am, I am your father, and you are magnates of the household, lay powers, secular persons. I refuse to hear your judgement.'[10] And with that he strode out, bearing his cross before him.

That evening, three of the bishops came to Henry and asked for permission for Becket to depart. Henry deferred a decision to the next day. Becket could take no more: that night he secretly fled south to the coast and two weeks later he had crossed the Channel and was in Flanders. We do not know whether Henry's men pursued him, and the crossing itself may have been slow, but it is not impossible that Henry had decided that whatever the difficulties of the archbishop being in exile, it might be the best solution. It was no novelty: Archbishop Anselm had gone into exile twice in his quarrel with Henry I half a century earlier, and Henry hoped that the pope might respond favourably to an appeal to his judgement. Unfortunately, Alexander sided with Becket when the case was heard at the end of November; he refused Becket's resignation, but took no action against Henry.

The next two years passed in a series of diplomatic man-oeuvres, until in June 1166, Becket finally lost patience with both the pope's hesitant approach and the continuing defi-ance of both Henry and the English bishops and officials: he excommunicated the leading royal officers, calling on Henry to repeal the articles set out at Clarendon. But the pope was not prepared to see a confrontation between king and archbishop, and the clergy remained loyal to Henry. By the end of the year, the king had persuaded Alexander to appoint legates to arbitrate. Becket's hands were tied because his authority over the English bishops was suspended by the pope, who feared a furious response from Becket to the news of the commission.

Henry also obtained permission from the pope to carry out another plan of his which Becket had obstructed by his flight to the continent. The king was anxious to secure the succession to the throne by having his eldest son, Prince Henry, crowned in his lifetime. By tradition, the Archbishop of Canterbury officiated at the coronation of an English king, but in the circumstances this was impossible. So Henry obtained a mandate from the pope which allowed Roger of Pont l'Évêque, Archbishop of York, the authority to crown his son, as he was not prepared to wait until the dispute with Becket had been resolved. This of course gave Becket a further grievance; he saw the move as a further erosion of his authority.

It was not until November 1167, over a year later, that the first meeting between the legates, Henry and Becket took place. Negotiations with the king and Becket were carried out separately, and the two adversaries did not meet face to face. Henry was in emotional mood: at the end of his first interview with the cardinals, he was reported (by one of Becket's supporters) as saying that he hoped he never set eyes on a cardinal again. At the end of the negotiations, on 5 December, he wept in public, begging the cardinals to persuade the pope to get rid of Becket, though the same onlooker reported that one of the cardinals could barely restrain his laughter.

A further year passed before the negotiations were reopened; two monks were appointed as the new legates in

May 1168, and in January 1169 king and archbishop met face to face for the first time in four years at a peace conference with the French at Montmirail. Both sides were ready to compromise, and Becket was almost persuaded by the legates to throw himself on the king's mercy, in return for Henry's withdrawal of the clause in the Clarendon articles forbidding appeals to the pope without royal permission. Becket further agreed not to include the clause 'saving God's honour', or 'saving his order', which had led to the breakdown of the Northampton meeting in 1164. But on his way to the ceremony of submission, one of his most fanatical supporters, Herbert of Bosham, persuaded him that he had to keep the clause simply in self-defence. Becket pronounced the fatal words 'saving God's honour' and despite long arguments he remained obstinate. Once more, the negotiations had failed.

Becket, who was living in relative poverty since no income from the see of Canterbury was reaching him and he was therefore dependent on charity from his sympathizers, now used his most drastic weapon again, and on Palm Sunday, 13 April 1169, excommunicated Gilbert Foliot, Bishop of London, the Bishop of Salisbury, the Earl of Norfolk and the head of the English branch of the Knights Templars, all of them strong supporters of the king. Henry, writing to Foliot, called this action 'the outrage which that traitor and enemy of mine, Thomas, has inflicted upon you and other subjects of my realm'.[11] This meant that the work of two cardinals, Gratian and Vivian, who had been appointed as the new mediators in February 1169 was very unlikely to succeed. They met the two sides separately in

July and August, but at the end of the second meeting with the king, Henry went off in a fury, swearing, 'By God's eyes, I would act differently if I were you.' Gratian's cool response was: 'Do not threaten us, my lord, for we fear no threats, coming from a court used to ruling emperors and kings.'[12]

Yet a week later, at a private meeting between Henry and the legates, the king succeeded in getting their agreement to the lifting of the excommunications. He then demanded that one of the legates should go to England to perform the necessary ceremony. When the cardinals refused, he strode out and mounted his horse, saying, 'Do what you like; I could not care less for you or your excommunications.'[13] At length he was pacified, and agreed to write to the pope offering terms for Becket; but he grew impatient again and declared that he would withdraw the proposal. Warned that the legates would take action against him, he replied, 'I know, I know; they will put an interdict on my lands. But if I can capture the strongest of castles in a day, can't I take one cleric who puts an interdict on me?' An interdict was the most fearsome ban in the Church's armoury: if an interdict on a country or a diocese was proclaimed, all churches would be closed and religious life would be suspended. Only baptism and the last rites would be allowed, except on the great feast days such as Christmas and Easter, and even then Mass would be said rather than sung. In a deeply religious age, it affected the entire population, and was a very powerful weapon.

Henry needed a solution to the problem of the excommunicates as soon as possible, and could not wait for the reply from Pope Alexander and Becket; his government would be severely hindered if his officials were prevented from doing their business – and excommunication would do just this, as Christians were expected to avoid all contact with anyone who had been excommunicated. So the negotiations were reopened; but at the end of two days of hard talking, Henry insisted on the inclusion of the phrase 'saving the dignity of his kingdom' in the letter offering peace. This direct echo of the archbishop's own defiant words would inevitably be rejected, and Henry, who seems by this time to have been highly temperamental, knew what the outcome would be. The negotiations dragged on through two further meetings, but were then abandoned.

Battle lines were now drawn up. Henry moved first, anticipating Becket's reaction. He decreed that all communication between England and the pope would be cut off. After 9 October, anyone carrying letters to or from the pope or Becket would be treated as a traitor. If any clergy obeyed an interdict pronounced by Becket, they would forfeit all their property. All clergy outside England were to return by 14 January 1170. Anyone coming from abroad was to be searched, and clerics with no royal permission to enter were to be sent back. Everyone in the kingdom was to swear to obey these articles, and furthermore, all men over twelve were to abjure Becket and the pope on oath.

Becket's response was, as Henry expected, to issue an interdict, to take effect on 2 February 1170 unless the king repented. Gratian returned to Alexander to report the failure of the legates' efforts, though soon after he had left, Cardinal Vivian held another meeting, during which the threats and counter-threats seemed to have brought both sides to reason. But once again, pride or personal animosity struck down the possibility of agreement. Henry, proclaiming that he had sworn never to give Becket the kiss of peace, refused this symbolic gesture which would have meant that Becket enjoyed his unconditional protection. Without that protection, Becket was in danger from his many enemies in England. Nothing would shift Henry on this, while the king himself was furious at his opponents' insistence on the ceremonial kiss. Yet there was at least a possibility that the next round of negotiations would succeed.

Henry himself was clearly very doubtful about this, for at this point the king brought into play his cherished plan to crown Prince Henry as co-ruler of England. It was nearly a decade since he had first mooted this, and he had the pope's letters allowing the Archbishop of York to do so, dating from three years earlier. So on 14 June 1170 at Westminster, the ceremony was carried out. Henry not only defied Becket on this occasion, but also King Louis of France, as Margaret, the prince's wife and Louis's daughter, was absent from the abbey. She would probably, in normal circumstances, have been crowned with her husband, and this was an insult to her and therefore to her father. Prince Henry, who was henceforth known as 'the young king', showed his true character, proud and quarrelsome, when his father served him at table after the ceremony. The Archbishop of York commented that no other prince in the world had such a distinguished servant, whereupon the young king replied, 'Why are you astonished? Shouldn't my father do this? He is of lower rank than me, as son of a queen and a duke, while I come from royal blood on both sides!'[14] It was a portent of storms to come.

The coronation resulted in a hardening of the pope's attitude to Henry, even though he had authorized the Archbishop of York to crown the young king. Alexander threatened an interdict on Henry's domains in France: Henry had prevented an interdict in England by cutting off communications across the Channel, but he could not prevent papal letters from reaching the Norman bishops. And because he had refused the kiss of peace to Becket, the archbishop could pose as the injured party. Practical politics now required that he should back down, if he was to avoid the disaster of an interdict. So at a meeting on the Norman border with France on 22 July, Henry offered the same terms as those that had been agreed with Cardinal Vivian. There was no mention of the kiss of peace, and Becket accepted this. His peace and security were guaranteed, and the offending clauses of the Clarendon declaration were to be annulled. At the end of the negotiations, which had taken place in the open air, Henry and Becket rode away from the rest of the company and talked alone for the first time in seven years. Becket gained Henry's consent to take action against the bishops who had participated in the coronation and had therefore infringed his rights as primate of England. At this, the archbishop dismounted and knelt before the king, but Henry held his stirrup for him to remount, saying with tears in his eyes: 'My lord archbishop, let us return to our old friendship, and each show the other what good he can; and let us forget our hatred completely.'[15] This was probably Henry's sincere desire; but too much had changed between them for the 'old friendship' to be viable again.

The impossibility of such a renewed friendship was quickly demonstrated. When the formal act of reconciliation took place at Amboise on 12 October, all went well until Becket came to attend Mass with the king, in the hope of receiving the kiss of peace during the service. Henry avoided the issue by ordering that a requiem Mass should be said, in which the kiss of peace is not exchanged. Becket now openly demanded this symbolic act of the king: Henry remained obstinate. When they parted at Chaumont-en-Vexin a few days later, Henry expressed his good wishes, and Becket is said to have replied: 'My lord, something tells me that I take leave of you now, never to see you again in this life.' Henry turned on him, saying, 'Do you think me a traitor?'[16] Becket's swift denial failed to appease the king, and Henry, having promised to escort the archbishop to England, wrote to say that matters of state had detained him. Becket returned to England alone.

Henry expected that in return for the concessions that he had made, Becket would similarly moderate his stance. By Christmas, it was clear that Becket was beyond compromise. As he left France, he had sent ahead letters which excommunicated the bishops who had taken part in the coronation. It is highly unlikely that Henry expected his permission to act against the bishops to be used in this way, because excommunication called into question the validity of the ceremony itself, and thus undermined the whole of Henry's plans for the succession. This was the moment that sealed the archbishop's fate: Henry's mood turned to fury when the bishops came to him at Argentan to protest against Becket's actions, and other messengers brought rumours of armed mobs at large in England under the arch-bishop's command. He summoned a council of his barons, and after a long and indecisive discussion, one of them could not restrain himself and told Henry: 'My lord, while Thomas lives, you will have no peace, nor quiet, nor pros-perity!'[17] The king was silent for a while, but his anger was obvious, and he finally burst out: 'What idle and miserable men I have encouraged and promoted in my kingdom, faithless to their lord, who let me be mocked by this low-born clerk!'[18] No one noticed the four knights who slipped quietly out of the company. When it was discovered that they had ridden to the coast, Henry realized what they intended to do, and gave orders that they should be stopped at any cost, and that Becket should be arrested.

The following days brought no news, until on New Year's Day 1171 a messenger rode into the castle at Argentan. He hesitated to go directly to the king, and instead told his news to the courtiers. They tried to put off the moment when Henry would learn of the disaster that had befallen him, but the arrival of the messenger could not be concealed from the king. It was as he had feared. The knights had taken ship for England before their pursuers could reach them. Once they landed, they went straight to Canterbury, where they confronted the archbishop and demanded that he should absolve the excommunicated bishops and stand trial in the king's court. Becket refused, and retreated into the cathedral, refusing to yield to the threat of force. The

knights drew their swords, and despite a desperate defence
by his clerks, cut down the archbishop in his own church,
in an unbelievable act of murder and sacrilege.

This was more than Henry could bear. He turned and left
the hall, and went to his chamber. He remained there for
three days, refusing food and speaking to no one, wracked
with grief as powerful as his anger had once been. All his
plans for a new order in England and for the security of his
lands were now in disarray, the plans which he had laid
long ago in the days of friendship with Becket, when he had
ridden and hunted and dreamed of a world where Church
and state would be at peace and working for the same ends.
Thomas Becket the clerk was dead and defeated: Thomas
Becket the martyr would conquer all Henry's dreams.

Henry had many other preoccupations during the years
when the quarrel with Becket seemed to overshadow everything else. It is easy to lose sight of the greater scheme
of which the controversial attempt at Clarendon to define
the Church's place in society was only part. We begin with
a second council at Clarendon nearly five years before
Becket's death, in early 1166. It has a much smaller place in
the history books, because there were no dramatic scenes
and the document that resulted, the 'Assize of Clarendon',
dealt fairly with a recognized problem, that of appeals from
local law courts. This was all part of Henry's objective, to
maintain public order in England, a task that baffled most
medieval kings.

Immediately after the end of the council, Henry crossed
to France. It was three years since he had last crossed the

Channel and in both his English and French domains this was a time of peace. Settlement of a rebellion in Brittany meant that Henry himself was able to enforce his claim to its overlordship, receiving the rebels' homage during the summer, and ensuring that his son Geoffrey was designated as heir to Brittany. It was the diplomatic high point of his reign: he had betrothed his daughter Matilda to one of the greatest lords of Germany, Henry the Lion, Duke of Saxony and Bavaria, four years earlier; and while he was at Mont St Michel on his journey through Brittany, the new King of Scotland, William the Lion, came to him and performed homage for his English lands. The following spring, Henry was able to purchase the overlordship of Toulouse, for which he had fought in vain eight years earlier.

This last manoeuvre was too much for Louis VII, who saw the power of his already over-mighty vassal as a major threat. Taking advantage of a quarrel between Henry and one of the vassals of Toulouse, the Count of Auvergne, Louis made an alliance with the count. Henry took pre-emptive action, invading the French lands to the south of Normandy after Easter 1167. A peace conference at Gisors on 4 June was to no avail, and Henry's military skills proved greater than those of the French. He captured Chaumont-en-Vexin, where the French supplies were being stored, and with it the Count of Champagne, while Louis's brother Henry was besieged in the citadel, unable to escape. In the exceptional heat of the summer, the French army suffered considerable losses as they retreated, many men dying of thirst. Louis agreed in August to a truce to last until the following Easter. This was highly opportune for Henry, as a further revolt had broken out in Brittany, and in September he marched against the rebels.

As Henry set out on this Breton campaign, his mother Matilda died at Rouen on 10 September 1167. She had been his mentor in statecraft after the death of his father, having played little part in his childhood when she was in England fighting to regain her kingdom. Matilda had suffered the treachery of the barons who had sworn to her father that they would support her, and knew that only steely determination and harsh measures would keep them in check. She was buried at the great Norman abbey of Bec, which had given England three archbishops of Canterbury, and had become a place symbolic of the links between Normandy and the English kingdom. Her latter years had been spent in charitable works, and Henry, absent when she died, distributed large sums in her memory to the Church and to the sick and poor.

Sporadic rebellions had been a feature of the politics of Eleanor's domains in Aquitaine. There had been trouble in Angoulême, where Eleanor's uncle, William Taillefer IV, was count, in the spring of 1167; this had been quickly suppressed by the local royal officers, but the following year there was a more serious revolt, in which he was joined by the counts of Marche and the lords of Lusignan, one of the most powerful families of the region. Henry took charge, and quickly seized the castle of Lusignan, destroying many of the rebels' other fortresses. But he had to return north to prepare for the end of the truce with the French, leaving Eleanor in charge with Patrick, Earl of Salisbury, as governor to assist her. No sooner had he gone than the Lusignans counter-attacked, seizing Patrick in an ambush. They then reached an agreement with Louis, and were able to prevent a treaty between Henry and Louis being signed in April 1168. All Henry could secure was a three-month truce; even this was welcome, since there was renewed trouble in Brittany. He was able to settle this, but the negotiations in the summer were unsuccessful, and fitful skirmishes continued on the Norman border until Christmas.

In January 1169, Henry and Becket met for the first time since 1165, at a conference at Montmirail. Here an agreement was successfully reached with the French king. This was confirmed in March, and settled in part the succession to Henry's domains on the continent, which fitted his scheme to ensure a smooth transition if he should die unexpectedly. Prince Henry became Count of Anjou and did homage for Anjou and Brittany to Louis's son Philip (who was only four at the time), as did his brother Richard for Aquitaine. Finally, Geoffrey did homage to Prince Henry for Brittany. Richard was betrothed to Louis's eight-year-old daughter Alice. All this seemed like a tidy and lasting arrangement, but like so many of these medieval family alliances designed to settle a quarrel between kings, it proved to be short-lived. The rivalry between Louis and his over-mighty vassal was too deep to be settled by even the cleverest of diplomats.

Henry did succeed in establishing Geoffrey as Duke of Brittany by the end of the year, and kept Christmas with him at Nantes. He crossed to England on 2 March 1170 and encountered a fierce storm in the Channel which scattered his fleet, sinking one ship. The rest made their way to the nearest ports on the English coasts. Henry himself reached Portsmouth on 3 March, though it was some time before the whereabouts of the other ships was known, and the French were convinced that Henry himself must have been drowned. This episode is a stark reminder of how difficult a Channel crossing could be: it is a recurrent theme in the history of the English kings with lands in France, and even in the nineteenth century the crossing was undertaken with some trepidation. Henry's uncle, William Audelin, heir to Henry I, was drowned in the famous *White Ship* disaster in 1120.

Henry's immediate objective in England was to deal with serious corruption on the part of his sheriffs, the officials in charge of what we now call counties. Early medieval government relied heavily on personal responsibility: the sheriffs took on their duties as tax collectors on the basis that they paid a fixed sum to the Exchequer, and then collected as much tax as they were entitled to in order to cover that sum. Unfortunately, this all too often became 'as much tax as they could', and in Henry's absence there had been widespread malpractice. In March, Henry ordered what one chronicler called 'a wonderful inquisition',[19] covering all accounts since 1166, to be completed by 14 June, a very short time for such an exercise.

This brings us to the point where, fatally, politics and Becket's intransigence collided, over the coronation of the young king, which took place on the same day that the inquisition was to be concluded. The repercussions of this political act led almost directly to Becket's death at the end of the year. That death, indeed martyrdom, immediately put Henry on the defensive, as the pope now authorized the severest measures against him, an interdict on his domains outside England and the personal excommunication of the king. An urgent embassy of the Norman bishops to Rome obtained only the cancellation of the king's sentence; however, papal legates were to be sent to Normandy to review the situation.

Maintaining the existing equilibrium in his continental lands in the face of the hostility of the French, and the natural rebelliousness of local lords unused to the rule of distant princes, was to occupy Henry for the remainder of his reign. But in the summer of 1171 he had one last project of conquest in mind to complete his lordship of the British Isles: to establish his rule over Ireland. His claim to the island went back to 1155, when he had obtained a grant from the pope making him Lord of Ireland, which he had never attempted to enforce.

Neither Wales nor Ireland was a united territory. Nominal authority over the other chieftains was claimed by different princes at different times in Wales; Owain, Prince of Gwynedd, was the nearest to an overlord in Henry's time, and after his death in 1166, Henry's authority was rarely challenged. In Ireland, where the title of *ard-rí* or high king was long established but usually meaningless, a similar loose federation of tribal leaders, each calling themselves king, was the nearest to centralized rule. There was no overall high king of all Ireland, save for a brief period in the early eleventh century: the kings of the south owed allegiance to the *ard-rí* based in Meath, while those of the

1. The image of kingship: Saul as portrayed by the artist who created the magnificent miniatures for the Winchester Bible in the middle of Henry II's reign. This is as near as we can get to Henry's physical appearance on state occasions.

2. Geoffrey of Anjou, Henry's father, from the enamel plaque which was hung above his tomb soon after his death in 1151. His device of four leopards is still a central element of the British royal coat of arms.

3. The three effigies of Plantagenet royalty in the great abbey at Fontevraud, where Eleanor of Aquitaine became a nun in 1203, and which was effectively the royal mausoleum of the family. The effigies are Eleanor in the foreground, Henry II in the centre, and Richard I in the background.

4. The east window of Poitiers Cathedral, showing Henry and Eleanor and their four sons at the foot of a crucifixion scene. The cathedral was begun by them in 1162, and the glass was probably installed before Henry's death.

6. The coronation of Henry the young king. After the ceremony, left, his father is shown on the right acting as cupbearer to his son.

5. Archbishop Thomas Becket and the two kings, Henry II and Louis VII, ride away in opposite directions after the failure of the negotiations at Montmirail in 1169; the kings gesture furiously at him, while Becket blesses the common people.

7. Eleanor of Aquitaine out hawking, a fresco from the chapel of St Radegund in Chinon, the subject of which is hotly debated. The most plausible suggestion is that it represents Richard I, on the right, with Eleanor and Richard's wife Berengaria (whom he married in 1191), and two squires, who could be Otto of Brunswick and John of Brittany, potential heirs to the Plantagenet domains.

8. Enamel plaque of Henry of Blois, Bishop of Winchester and brother of King Stephen, showing him presenting an altar to an unknown church. He played an important role in Henry's reign up to his death in 1171.

MARS AVRO GEMOTS QO PRIOR OMNIBVS AVTOR: DONA DAT HENRICVS VIVVS IN BREDE
DILIMENTE PAREM MVSISTMAR CO VOCE PRIOREM: FAMA VIRIS MO EIS CONCILIANT SVPEROS

HENRICVS ✠ EPISCOP

9. Henry II does penance at the tomb of Thomas Becket, an image from the stained glass at Canterbury Cathedral, installed in the magnificent new Gothic cathedral begun in 1174 and completed in 1220.

north acknowledged the *ard-rí* based in Ulster. In both territories, local quarrels were common; and it was one of these local quarrels in Ireland that drew Henry into the project of conquest.

Around 1150, Dermot MacMurrough, Prince of Leinster, had expanded his power by alliances with two other princes. This led him into a prolonged confrontation with Tiernan O'Rourke, King of Breffny, whose lands stretched across Ireland to the north of Connaught, and who was also ambitious to extend his principality. In 1166 he and his allies drove MacMurrough out of Leinster, and MacMurrough fled to Aquitaine, seeking Henry, who, although he personally refused to help him, allowed him to seek support from any of his barons who were prepared to offer it. MacMurrough eventually came to an agreement with Richard de Clare, Earl of Pembroke, one of the most powerful of the Welsh marcher lords, who guarded the borders or 'marches' of Wales. In return for his daughter's hand in marriage and the inheritance of Leinster on his death, MacMurrough persuaded him to invade the following spring. De Clare had agreed provided he could obtain Henry's specific consent, which he only requested two years later. It was about the beginning of May 1169 that the first Norman troops landed near Wexford. Their leader was Robert Fitzstephen, and the whole force comprised only 400 foot soldiers, 30 knights, 60 mailed horsemen and 300 archers. The Irish had no cavalry, and nothing to rival the Welsh longbow, and MacMurrough was quickly reinstated in Leinster. Not content with this, and encouraged by his almost instant success, he now plotted to seize the high kingship from the incumbent,

Rory O'Connor, and succeeded in taking Dublin, Ireland's commercial and political capital with the help of de Clare himself, who landed in Ireland in August 1170.

It was at this point that Henry himself intervened. If de Clare was successful in Ireland, and became the effective master of Leinster, he might well declare himself an independent prince in Wales as well, and Henry therefore sent letters to him and to his fellow Normans in Ireland, ordering them to return or forfeit their estates in Wales and England. Their response was to send one of their number as an emissary to Henry, as they were now besieged in Dublin by the Irish, who had enlisted the help of Norsemen settled in Ireland, descendants of the Vikings who had established Dublin in the ninth century. The Normans made a daring sortie, and were able to annihilate the Irish and Viking troops, leaving them free to seize the rest of the towns on the eastern coast. De Clare was able to negotiate with Henry from a strong position, and surrendered the three major towns, Dublin, Wexford and Waterford, in return for the actual lordship of Leinster and the retention of his Welsh and English lands.

Henry was already in Wales when this settlement was reached. He had to wait for six weeks for a favourable wind, and spent the time strengthening his alliances in Wales. His former enemy Rhys ap Griffith met him and offered him 300 horses, 4,000 oxen and 24 hostages as a token of friendship and alliance. He was granted Cardigan and other lands in south Wales in exchange, while Henry returned all but thirty-six of the horses as a reciprocal gesture. The king also, as was his habit during such enforced delays, went on pilgrimage, to St David's. Here he made an offering of two velvet choristers' caps and a handful of silver; when the bishop invited him to dinner, he would not accept an elaborate meal, but dined standing with his escort, before riding sixteen miles over the mountains to Pembroke in the darkness and heavy rain. He embarked from Milford Haven on 16 October 1171 and landed near Waterford two days later.

Henry brought 400 knights with him, and perhaps 4,000 men in all, the most powerful army yet seen in Ireland. De Clare met him to surrender the three towns, and the first of the Irish princes who were to submit to their new overlord also arrived, Dermot MacCarthy of Desmond. Equally important was a meeting at Lismore with the papal legate for Ireland. Henry's title to Ireland depended on the pope's grant of 1155, and there was mutual interest in collaboration. The Irish Church, despite its spirituality and superb cultural heritage in the monasteries, was largely disorganized, resistant to central authority and wedded to the old and anarchic rule of the Celtic past, where local customs, sometimes of pagan origin, still persisted. Henry and the legate, Christian O'Conarchy, agreed that a great council of the Irish Church should be held to put into effect the reforms which had been agreed as long ago as 1139.

During that autumn, all the southern kings except Rory O'Connor himself did homage to Henry; O'Connor may have submitted to him, but does not seem to have done homage. Henry made no attempt to subdue the Ulster kings, and indeed Ulster was to remain fiercely independent of the English kings throughout the medieval period. Henry kept his Christmas court at Dublin in a palace built in the native style, from wattle and daub, but in his usual splendour: just as the Norman cavalry had astounded the Irish troops two years before, so the magnificence of the English king astonished the Irish princes who came to the celebrations.

The Church council that had been agreed in the previous autumn opened at Cashel on 2 February 1172. Reforms were enacted to bring the Irish Church into line with the rituals and laws established throughout Western Christendom. The final clause stated that, if in doubt, matters should be conducted according to the practices of the Church in England. In return, Henry granted the clergy the immunities and privileges enjoyed by the English clergy, and was able to secure their agreement that his overlordship of Ireland on the basis of the papal grant of 1155 was valid. Furthermore, they swore an oath of fealty to him. All this was politically very valuable. Amid the shifting sands of Irish politics the clergy were a reliable and influential presence, and this agreement would be more effective than any of the alliances with the kings.

Henry had effectively put on hold the struggle with the pope over the consequences of Becket's murder by retreating to the furthest reaches of his domains. But the showdown could not be delayed for ever, and in his absence there were rumours of a conspiracy among his sons. Messages from papal legates on the continent had also reached him, demanding that he meet them. There was little more he could do in Ireland, and he prepared to return to England at the beginning of March 1172. As so often, bad weather

delayed the crossing, and it was six anxious weeks before
he was able to embark, on 17 April. It took only a day's
sailing to reach Wales; leaving Wexford at dawn, he was at
St David's by nightfall. Henry knew he must now act
quickly, and after conferring with his ministers at Winchester, he reached the papal legates at Gorron in Maine just a
month after he had left Ireland. He had covered two sea
crossings and eight hundred miles on land in this time, with
a speed that seemed to his contemporaries diabolic: they
said that the King of England flew rather than rode.

Henry now had to face the consequences of the murder
of Becket, and in particular the extent of his personal
involvement in the sequence of events that had led up to it.
The shock with which the news of the archbishop's killing
had been received meant that Becket was almost immediately venerated as a saint: miracles were already attributed
to him, while Henry himself was cast as the villain, responsible for the disaster even if he had not directly ordered it.
Even Henry of Blois, the aged Bishop of Winchester, who
had been one of the crucial supporters of Matilda and her
son during Stephen's reign, saw the king as deeply impli-
cated in what had happened. When, in the weeks before he
left for Ireland, Henry went to see him on his deathbed, the
bishop bitterly accused him of causing Becket's death. This
was one of Henry's friends; his enemies in France and in the
papal entourage had no doubt of his guilt.

Henry met the papal legates at Gorron on 16 May 1172,
and exchanged the formal kiss of peace with them. The
negotiations began the next day at Savigny, and many
points were agreed; but Henry refused to give the legates

the full powers in England that they demanded, wary of what they might do. All he would say was that they could go anywhere they wished in his domains. He left the meeting maintaining that his long absence had been quite justified, since the legates were demanding the impossible. But the legates were not going to give up. Another meeting was arranged at Avranches for the following day, and terms were agreed. Because Henry's eldest son was now jointly king with his father, he too had to be present to sign the settlement, and on his arrival on Sunday 21 May, the ceremonial oath by which Henry cleared himself of guilt and the sentence of penance were carried out. At the north doorway of the cathedral, facing the legates, Henry swore with one hand on the Gospels that he had neither desired nor ordered the murder of Thomas Becket, Archbishop of Canterbury, and that the news had caused him more grief than joy. In a typical spontaneous addition, he swore that he had not mourned the death of his father or of his mother so much as that of Becket. However, he acknowledged that he had unintentionally caused Becket's death by his display of fury in the royal court at Argentan, and would therefore carry out whatever penance or other stipulation the legates might make.

In public the legates set out their conditions for reparation. Henry was to send a contingent of 200 knights to Palestine, equipped according to the standard required by the Knights Templars. All 'evil customs' introduced in his reign, and particularly the clauses of the Constitutions of Clarendon to which the pope objected, were to be withdrawn. The possessions of the see of Canterbury were to be restored and compensation paid for any lost revenue. And finally, if the pope thought it necessary, Henry was to go in person to Spain to fight the Saracens. Further to this, there were secret clauses which specified the penance to be carried out by the king personally, namely fasts and the giving of alms. And both Henry and the young king were to swear that they would be faithful to Alexander and his successors as pope, a vital clause in view of Henry's threats in the past to switch his allegiance to Victor IV.

Henry had succeeded in presenting his case: he was wrongfully accused as to his responsibility for the murder, and the only blame that attached to him was that of having accidentally inspired others to carry it out. Throughout the negotiations, moreover, he had shown no signs of subservience to the Church, treating the legates as equals, not his superiors. He declared to the legates, 'My lords legate, my body is in your hands; I am prepared to go wherever you command, to Jerusalem, Rome or Compostela, if you so wish,' presenting this as something he offered of his own free will.[20] And it was specifically of his own free will that the king was then led to the cathedral door to receive the absolution before he went in to hear Mass.

The reconciliation of the king had to be made public in an age when news travelled slowly and unreliably, and two further ceremonies were required, at Caen on 30 May and back at Avranches on 28 September, four weeks after the papal bull announcing the reconciliation had been issued. It only remained to carry out the terms of the agreement, and here Henry largely had his own way. Instead of the force of 200 knights destined for the East, the king was able to substitute the founding of three religious houses, which he did, though rather half-heartedly. On the most important matter, the question of retracting the 'evil customs' introduced in his reign and enshrined in the Constitutions of Clarendon, Henry had his own ideas. He wrote to the Bishop of Exeter at the end of May 1172 telling him about the settlement and saying that it had been stipulated that he should abolish 'those customs prejudicial to the churches of your territories which have been introduced in your time', but that 'I reckon [these] to be few or none'.[21] This had been his argument throughout the controversy: in line with the medieval horror of innovation, Henry had always held that he was simply reaffirming existing practices which had fallen into abeyance. In fact, his concept of the existing practices was a new interpretation of old customs; but the same was equally true of the Church's views. Both sides were pressing claims to new ground, while pretending that they were merely setting out the status quo.

On two crucial points, however, Henry made no headway. The first was that of the immunity of the clergy from trial in royal courts. This had not been entirely straightforward before Becket's death. Even the commentaries on the great lawbook of the Church, Gratian's *Decretum*, were uncertain about this issue. Pope Alexander himself had written on the subject and had appeared to justify the idea of trial in the Church's courts, which, if it resulted in the loss of clerical status for the individual concerned, could be followed by a secular trial. But after Becket's death, his view hardened and he decreed instead that there should not be a secular trial in such circumstances, thus enshrining Becket's position in the Church's law code.

The second point was the question of appeals to the pope. These could constitute a challenge to the king's sovereignty, and hence Henry was anxious to control them. In most cases, the appeals were concerned with purely ecclesiastical matters, and it was only those which might challenge royal rights or secular law that Henry wished to prevent – indeed, he and his successors used appeals to the pope for their own purposes – and so a complete ban was out of the question. The problem arose where canon law might conflict with secular law; in such cases the pope might issue a decree without any reference to the king which took no account of the existing secular law. But if there was no possibility of such appeals, the ultimate authority became the Archbishop of Canterbury, and this could be equally dangerous to royal wishes. In practice, although Henry had to yield to the pope on this issue, selective bans on appeals to Rome were exercised and this continued into the fourteenth century, usually enforced by watching the ports from which messengers or individuals might embark on such a journey.

No sooner had Henry settled his differences with the Church than new dangers loomed. Indeed, the Christmas of 1172 marks the apogee of Henry's rule, with his domains at peace, administered according to his wishes by a newly created class of royal officials. The future seemed prosperous. The illusion was soon broken, however: once again, the trouble came from those closest to him. It was now his own family, as proud and ambitious as he was himself, who rebelled against his close hold on power. The coronation of the young king, designed to ensure the succession, proved to have been a mistake: with the title of king, the younger Henry had anticipated that he would be given real power. While his father was in Ireland, there had been rumours of plots in which he was involved, and early in 1173 he had taken umbrage when, in negotiations for his brother John's marriage to the daughter of the Count of Maurienne, the king had offered three castles as John's share of his lands. Why should John have lands, when he, as king, had none? He refused to ratify the agreement as Henry's heir, and the treaty was signed on Henry's word alone.

When Henry and his son returned to Normandy, the rift between them had become acute. Henry decided after some deliberation to remove men in the young king's entourage whom he suspected of fomenting his eldest son's ambition to rule in his own right. However, when the knights in question were dismissed at Chinon in early March, the young king slipped out of the castle, having made the guards drunk, and rode a hundred miles to Alençon and then to Argentan. His father pursued him; the young king's original intention may have been to cross the Channel and raise a rebellion in England, but he now headed for Paris, to seek the support of his father-in-law, Louis. And Henry soon received news that a number of barons had declared their support for his son.

The next blow for Henry was the desertion of his sons Richard and Geoffrey, apparently at their mother's urging. Eleanor herself attempted to reach Paris, disguised as a man, to the horror of her contemporaries, but was brought back in disgrace to spend the next decade in prison. Henry had distributed titles – Richard was Duke of Aquitaine and Geoffrey Duke of Brittany – but had kept a tight grip on the power that might have gone with the titles. Although this may seem a sudden storm within Henry's family, it is all about power: the children of two such ambitious and able rulers as Henry and Eleanor chafed at the bit about the way their father kept everything under his own personal control. Henry's sons failed to realize that, without that tight control, the Angevin empire was impossible to rule.

When the young king arrived in Paris, Louis saw this as his great opportunity to weaken the threatening power of the Angevins. As crowned King of England, the younger Henry was able to make grants of land to his supporters, though they would have to use force to obtain them as his father would not recognize such grants. He could also counter his father's wishes and obstruct his plans because of his new status as co-ruler of England. Louis encouraged him in all this, and provided him with a new seal for these purposes. He also made the great lords of France swear to support the young king in his warfare, and in return they received great fiefs: for example, Philip, Count of Flanders, was given Kent, including Dover and Rochester castles and an income of £1,000 a year. In return for the allegiance of William, King of Scotland, young Henry granted him all the lands north of the Tyne, while the Scottish king's brother David was given Cambridgeshire. All this would have seriously weakened the royal power in England, and indeed laid it open to Scottish incursions. The young king was only looking to the moment, while Louis was using him to pave the way for a future in which his son-in-law would be powerless against the might of France. And on the political front, the young king prevented the election of a new Archbishop of Canterbury to replace Thomas Becket: he appealed to the pope on the grounds that the election needed his royal approval, at the same time promising that he would repeal the Constitutions of Clarendon and allow the English Church full freedom.

Henry II shrewdly guessed that this unnatural Anglo-French alliance would not hold together, and spent his time largely in Normandy, where he hunted rather than raising an army; but he was certainly watching events closely and was deliberately letting it be known that he thought nothing of the threats issuing from Paris. And when war did come in May 1173, fortune was on his side. The brother of Philip of Flanders, Matthew of Boulogne, was killed in the first weeks of the campaign: exactly five years before, he had sworn an oath of fealty to Henry. Philip himself took fright at this apparently divine retribution, and returned to Flanders, perhaps partly because he suspected that the campaign was not going to be successful. Indeed, his withdrawal made failure almost certain, as his support was vital if the young king was to make any impression on the well-organized Norman duchy, whose forces, even without Henry himself in the field, were well able to resist the attackers.

Louis had been besieging the town of Verneuil, on the southern border of Normandy, and the inhabitants had agreed to surrender on 9 August if no relief force appeared: their lives and goods were to be spared. Henry came within seven miles of the town on 8 August, and, threatened by the possibility of a pitched battle, Louis proposed a truce until the next day, followed by peace talks at Conches, thirty miles away. Henry withdrew, but Louis scandalously made this a pretext not only to demand the surrender of Verneuil, but also to sack the town against his previous agreement and take the inhabitants prisoner. Henry, furious at the deception, pursued the French without success, and then turned back to Rouen. A fortnight later, Henry had better news from Brittany. The rebellion there had been led by Ralph de Fougères and William Patrick, Earl of Salisbury: they had bribed their way into the town of Dol, and Henry's mercenary troops from Brabant had been driven out. However, the latter regrouped and counter-attacked: the earl was captured and the other leaders of the rebellion forced to take refuge in the castle. Henry responded with one of his characteristic lightning strikes: he covered the two hundred miles to Dol in a little over two days, ordered siege engines to be constructed and took the castle three days later. Ralph and sixty-eight other nobles were seized and imprisoned, and the revolt in Brittany was at an end.

It was clear that Henry was not an opponent to be treated lightly, and that the alliances and promises on which the young king relied might not be enough to defeat him. Henry had no wish for a prolonged war, however, and a peace conference was arranged on 25 September at Gisors, the traditional meeting place for negotiations between the French and English kings. Henry offered almost ridiculous amounts of money – half the royal revenues in England for the young king, and the same in Aquitaine for Richard – but what his sons wanted was a say in the politics and government of the Angevin realms. This Henry would not concede at any price, as a division of power would threaten the cherished peace and order he had brought to his domains, and so the conference broke up.

The young king had another reason for not wanting to settle with his father at this point. He knew that an invasion force of cavalry and Flemish mercenaries under his supporter the Earl of Leicester was on its way to England; indeed, the earl landed near Felixstowe at about the time that the conference at Gisors broke up. He made his way to the fortress of his ally Hugh Bigod at Framlingham, but his troops damaged Bigod's lands en route and he had to move on towards his stronghold in Leicester. That town had been taken from the rebels on 3 July by Henry's officers, though the castle held out. The earl had hoped to assemble troops in Suffolk before he set out, and his army was small. The leaders of the English government, Richard Lucy and Humphrey Bohun, summoned an army to gather at Bury St Edmunds, and intercepted Leicester at Fornham, just north of the town. Here they overwhelmed the cavalry and slaughtered the Flemish mercenaries, the local peasants joining in with pitchforks and scythes. The Earl of Leicester and his knights were captured, and the royal officers were able to put in place garrisons to counter anything that Hugh Bigod might do in East Anglia: this obliged him to seek a truce, the terms being that he send his own force of Flemish mercenaries home.

A truce was also agreed in France to last until the end of March 1174, and even when it expired there was only desultory fighting. The young king and Louis decided to try to raise the revolt in England again, since William of Scotland – who had refused young Henry's offer of an allegiance and was fighting on his own account – had invaded England with some success, seizing a number of fortresses. An army was raised in Yorkshire, and was following William as he retreated in face of this opposition. On 13 July, Henry II was at Canterbury, doing penance for his part in Becket's murder: at dawn he was kneeling in prayer before the archbishop's tomb, having passed the night fasting after a ritual scourging by the monks the previous day. At almost the exact moment when the rites were completed, the Scottish invasion came to an end, outside Alnwick three hundred miles to the north. A group of four hundred English knights had ridden ahead of the English army to reconnoitre, including the leaders of the expedition. A sudden mist had enveloped them the previous evening and they had wandered all night, unable to find their bearings. When the fog lifted at dawn, they were initially horrified to find that they were outside the walls of Alnwick and that the whole Scottish army lay before them. The only way out was to launch a surprise attack: helped by the Scots' initial mistake of thinking that they were a returning party of raiders from their own army, they charged the Scottish nobles who were scrambling to arm and mount their horses. William's horse was killed under him, and he surrendered to Henry's justiciar, Ranulf de Glanvill. The remaining Scottish nobles were either killed or captured. It was, in the view of the monks at Canterbury when the news reached the south a week later, a miracle brought about by the saint because of Henry's penance: no coincidence, but Becket's intervention.

With this, the rebellion in England collapsed. The young king, who had been waiting for a favourable wind for several weeks in order to cross from Gravelines near Calais, returned to Normandy and joined Louis in an attempt to take Rouen. The town was very strongly defended, and after a fortnight he had made no headway. On St Lawrence's Day, 10 August, there was the traditional truce to mark the feast day of an important saint: the gates were opened and the citizens poured out to join in sports and games on the opposite bank of the Seine from Louis's army. The French king's nobles urged him to take advantage of the unguarded state of the city to seize it; at first he was reluctant, but eventually he told the army to assemble silently for the attack. As they moved forward, a monk saw them and rang the great bell of the abbey to warn his fellow citizens. They rapidly returned and closed the gates, and Louis's men were driven off. Two days later, Henry reached Rouen, cut off the French army's supplies and made preparations to attack them from within the town. At this Louis retreated, and sent envoys to propose a meeting, to which Henry agreed as long as he was free to pursue Richard, who was still upholding the rebellion in Poitou. A little over a month later, Richard too had been brought to heel, and on 23 September came to his father professing deep repentance and offering his submission.

Six days later, a meeting on the Loire near Tours brought the effective surrender of the young king and his followers. Henry, as victor, could dictate the terms and, in financial matters, was almost as generous as he had been in his earlier, rejected offer. A general amnesty was proclaimed, with William of Scotland and the Earls of Leicester and Chester the only exceptions, and all estates forfeited by the rebels were to be returned to the king. But no political power was transferred to Henry's sons, and the treaty was silent as to the fate of their mother, Eleanor, whom Henry regarded as one of the ringleaders of the revolt.

The uprising had been costly, but Henry did make one important gain out of the events of the previous year. William of Scotland had to do homage for his kingdom, and all his vassals had to swear loyalty to Henry; his brother David was to be hostage for the treaty, and five great castles were to have English garrisons, including those at Stirling and Berwick. Furthermore, the Scottish Church was to be subject to the Archbishop of Canterbury. It seemed that the great rebellion was at an end.

What remained, however, were the underlying causes of the revolt. As a result, the history of the rest of Henry's reign is in many ways a replay on a lesser scale of the events of 1173–4. The impossibility, from Henry's stubborn viewpoint, of sharing power with his sons in any meaningful way continued to poison his relationship with them, and the quarrel seethed in their minds, occasionally boiling over into action. That action, usually quickly quelled by Henry, was interspersed with tearful reconciliations between father and sons, a reminder of the turbulent spirit of the Plantagenet family that contrasted so sharply with Henry's severe and rational approach to government.

A typical example of these vagaries occurred in March 1175 when Henry, having settled matters to his satisfaction in France, proposed to return to England and summoned the young king to go with him. Louis's courtiers had persuaded the latter that his father intended to imprison him if he crossed the Channel, and he refused to obey his father's orders. Henry guessed what had happened, and sent a conciliatory message in reply: the outcome was the arrival of the young king to be reconciled with his father, weeping and protesting his loyalty; he renewed his homage for his lands in England and Normandy. For the next two months, the two kings travelled together, and on 28 May they both visited Canterbury to give thanks to Becket, in what was the young king's first sight of the saint's elaborate tomb. When, the following month, at a council at Woodstock, Henry forbade any of those who had rebelled against him to appear at court unless he summoned them, the young king does not appear to have objected. Father and son spent over a year largely in each other's company, but even if he shared in some of the decisions made during this time, the young king eventually grew restive and wished to return to his old friends who were now banned from court. He asked permission to go on a pilgrimage to Compostela, but Henry realized that this was just an excuse to go abroad and allowed him to go only as far as Normandy. Yet although Henry took precautions against a new rebellion in September 1176, there were no real signs of dissension in the course of the next four years.

The reason for this was that the young king had largely abandoned his political ambitions, and was thoroughly enjoying himself in a long succession of great tournaments, then a relatively new sport, in northern France and Flanders. His mentor was William Marshal, once a squire in the retinue of the Earl of Salisbury and, although the son of a minor Wiltshire knight, he was a man of exceptional character and abilities who was to end his career as regent of England during the minority of Henry III in the 1220s. As a companion of the young king, and a very skilled tourneyer, he was a leading figure in the development of chivalric ideals in the second half of the twelfth century.

In 1180, Louis became seriously ill and incapable of ruling, due to a stroke. His son Philip took over, and was crowned in September when his father died. Philip was a much stronger character than his father, and took as his mission the reduction of English power in France. He also imitated many of Henry's methods, and in so doing decided to ban tournaments held without royal permission, following a similar ban in England under Henry I. The fashion for tournaments declined, now that permission was needed, and in 1181 we find the young king helping Philip in a war against the Count of Flanders. At about this time, William Marshal fell out of favour with him; there were slanderous stories about an affair between him and the young king's wife, Margaret, and he found it prudent to go on a pilgrimage to Jerusalem, since Henry II was equally hostile to him. At Christmas in 1182, the king and his sons held a splendid court at Caen, then at New Year Henry, perhaps trying to placate his eldest son, made Geoffrey do homage to the young king for Brittany, and the ceremony was duly performed. He then turned to Richard and asked him to do the same for the duchy of Aquitaine, but Richard had a quarrel with the young king about a castle at Clairvaux, which the latter claimed stood on land belonging to him. As a result, Richard refused to do homage to his brother.

The next round of civil war took place in the spring of 1183 between the young king and Geoffrey on the one side, and Richard on the other. When it became apparent that Richard was likely to lose, Henry intervened at Easter and besieged the young king in Limoges, where the latter is said to have ordered his archers to take aim deliberately at Henry. The young king soon submitted, as did Geoffrey, but in both cases this was feigned, and they at once set out to maraud in the rest of Richard's domains. Geoffrey actually plundered the Abbey of St Martial in Limoges itself, while the young king did the same at the Abbey of Rocamadour, where the legendary sword of the hero Roland was said to be: he was accused of taking it and replacing it with his own. Within a few days, however, he contracted a fever and rapidly declined. He summoned his father, who suspected a trick after his earlier behaviour and refused to come, though he sent a prelate with a ring which had once belonged to Henry I. On June 7, the young king made his confession, once in private and once before his knights. His last message to his father asked for mercy for his supporters, and for Queen Eleanor and Queen Margaret. He died aged twenty-six, lying on a bed of ashes with a stone at his head and one at his feet, covered by the crusader's cloak as a reminder of a vow he had never fulfilled. By his side was William Marshal, restored to favour and now charged with carrying out the vow on his master's behalf. The young king's crimes were quickly forgotten, and poets celebrated instead his reputation for knightly prowess. William Marshal was the messenger who took the news to the king. Henry, he later told his biographer, had simply replied, 'I trust in God for his salvation,' and when asked to provide a sum of money to settle the young king's debts, Henry did so, remarking, 'My son has cost me much more than that, and would that he were still costing me!'[22]

If the relations between Henry and his eldest son had been difficult, at least Henry had the upper hand. The young king had charm and the ability to win people over, but lacked political skill; he had never fought a war on his own account, even on a small scale. His brother Richard was a different matter; that Henry did not underestimate the danger that he presented is shown by his first action towards Richard after the latter had become heir to the throne: the confiscation of all his castles in Poitou. If this was because he knew how attached Richard was to Aquitaine as a whole, his next move was a serious misjudgement. He needed to make new arrangements for his remaining sons, and his solution was to give Richard the domains held by the young king – England, Normandy and Anjou – with overlordship of the rest of the Angevin lands, and to make John ruler of Aquitaine, holding it from Richard just as Geoffrey was to hold Brittany. Richard's response made his feelings clear: he retreated to Poitou, and sent a message that he would never surrender Aquitaine. Henry did not press the matter, but a year later, having released Eleanor from her semi-captivity and restored her to favour, he

ordered Richard to hand over the duchy to his mother.
Richard could not gainsay this: he had ruled severely in the
duchy, and had successfully subdued unruly barons who
now remembered Eleanor with affection, and he knew that
he could raise a revolt against his father, but not against his
mother, to whom Aquitaine actually belonged.

Philip was more skilful than Louis had been in wooing
Henry's sons. Geoffrey succumbed to his blandishments in
August 1186, but died of injuries suffered in a tournament
while at the French court. While Philip seems to have genuinely cared for him, the general verdict was that Geoffrey was
the least appealing of Henry's sons, possessing Henry's energy
but misdirecting it, and Henry's eloquence but misusing it: in
short, a successful troublemaker. In 1187, less than a year
later, after a brief war with France provoked by a minor border incident, Richard was the next to go to the court at Paris.
Although he had undertaken one successful campaign against
the Count of Toulouse, he, like his elder brother, had no formal power of his own. Soon he and Philip were 'eating from
the same dish and sleeping in the same bed',[23] and Richard
took a crusader's oath without his father's consent. Henry
ignored all this, and when they met at Angers, the two were
reconciled and Richard renewed his homage.

In the same year, both Henry and Philip took the cross in
response to the news of the destruction of the Christian
army in Palestine at the Battle of Hattin. This meant that
there had to be a truce between them, as it was sacrilege to
attack a crusader's lands. But the old quarrel between the
dukes of Aquitaine and Raymond, Count of Toulouse,
flared up again: in revenge for Richard's victory the

previous year, Count Raymond seized and maimed some Poitevin merchants, and Richard retaliated by invading his lands and capturing the knight who had advised the count to attack the merchants. Raymond responded by capturing two English knights going on pilgrimage to Compostela, and Philip now intervened, ordering the count to give them up. Without waiting for Philip's permission, Richard invaded Toulouse itself.

The French king seems to have decided to take this as a pretext for renewed war, and it was he who breached the crusading truce in June 1188. The pattern of events from here on indicates a mixture of both cold calculation and impetuous anger. Even the usually cool-headed Philip could give way to rage: at a meeting at Gisors in hot weather in late September 1188, Henry and his entourage sat in the shade of the tree where such meetings were traditionally held, while Philip and his men sweltered in the sun. When Henry left, a furious Philip ordered the tree to be cut down, as if to say that there would be no more negotiations, only war.

The fighting was, as usual, inconclusive, though the Counts of Flanders and Blois, Philip's chief allies, refused to attack Henry since he was now a crusader. When it came to negotiations, Philip would play along and agree a settlement, and then add a totally unacceptable condition at the last minute. After one such meeting, in early October, Richard decided to play his own hand and act without consulting Henry. He offered to settle the original cause of the war by submitting the quarrel between himself and Count Raymond to Philip's judgement, thus throwing away one of

Henry's chief bargaining points. At the next conference, he objected to the terms of mutual restoration of lands, as he would lose a valuable province, Quercy, in return for two castles which would bring in no revenue. Then, in what seems like a typical outburst of Angevin temper, he turned to his father and demanded that his marriage to Philip's half-sister Alice should be celebrated. Alice had been in Henry's keeping for the last ten years, and there were rumours later that Henry had seduced her. These may have been put about later by Richard, when he no longer wished to marry her, but the challenge was something that was intended to rankle with Henry. Even worse was the next demand, that there should be a ceremony of homage to him as heir to the Angevin lands. This Henry was prepared to do when it suited him, but not in a situation where it would seem that it had been performed under pressure from France. Richard compounded matters by doing homage to Philip for all the lands his father held, without infringing his father's right to hold them during his lifetime and the homage he owed his father. When the young king had rebelled, the prospect of his coming to the throne had been remote. Now Henry was fifty-six, and his health was declining: he was seriously ill during the winter. It was likely that Richard would be king within quite a short space of time, and potential rebels were inclined to take this into account. One more conference, called by the pope in his anxiety that the crusade should not be prevented by a war between England and France, was held on the Norman border at the beginning of June 1189. Despite the presence of the papal legate, and his threat of an interdict against Philip, no settlement was reached. Richard and the French struck quickly, and Henry was unprepared. He was at Le Mans, with only a handful of men, and did his best to secure the city from attack, blocking all the fords across the river: but the French entered by an old crossing that had been forgotten, and set fire to the suburbs. Henry's luck had at last run out. The wind blew the flames inside the walls, and the town was soon on fire. The king and about seven hundred knights retreated towards Fresnay – a retreat which was more of a flight, something that had never happened to Henry before. Richard, in hot pursuit, had not armed himself, and found himself confronting William Marshal, now in Henry's service. Richard was at William's mercy, and begged him not to kill him; William replied, 'Indeed I won't. Let the Devil kill you!' and plunged his spear into Richard's horse instead.[24]

Henry's winter illness now recurred and he took refuge at Chinon at the end of June. At a peace conference arranged near Tours on 4 July, he was also suffering from blood poisoning from a wound in his heel and had to be supported on his horse. Philip's demands were humiliating, but with Richard at his enemy's side he had no choice other than submission. As he gave the kiss of peace to Richard as token of his acceptance of the terms, he muttered, 'God grant that I may not die until I have had my revenge on you.'[25] He returned to Chinon, where next day a messenger came with the news that John too, said to be his favourite son, had gone over to Richard. At this he gave up, turning his face to the wall, and crying: 'Now let everything go as it will; I care no longer for myself or anything else in the world.' And when the next day he was carried into the chapel of Chinon Castle to receive extreme unction, his last words were: 'Shame, shame on a conquered king.'[26] He died almost alone, and William Marshal had to arrange a makeshift funeral. Then the body was borne to the Abbey of Fontevraud, across the forest to the south, which he had named as his burial place.

That night, a lone horseman dismounted at the church door. It was Richard. He came into the broad nave and walked up to the choir where his father's body lay. The nuns knelt in prayer around the bier; Richard stood by them, unmoving and seemingly unmoved, 'for as long as it takes to say "Our Father"',[27] before looking at his father's face for the last time. He knelt briefly, then rose and left the church as quickly and quietly as he had come.

# 3
# His Achievements

Henry created an empire of his own. He was King of England, overlord of Scotland and Ireland and much of Wales. In France he was overlord of Brittany, ruler of Normandy, Anjou, Maine and Aquitaine, the last through his marriage to Eleanor, and overlord of Toulouse. His power stretched from the furthest parts of the British Isles almost to the Mediterranean, and he overshadowed the French king in his own kingdom. Yet it was to prove an ephemeral wonder. There was no central administration, and no organized structure to it: what linked these wide lands together was the person of Henry himself. If he had any vision of its survival, it was as a kind of federation to be ruled by his heirs, with their relationship to each other as the binding force. His overwhelming desire to retain power in his own hands and the tensions and jealousies that resulted meant that the necessary relationships were never built in his lifetime. Richard's absence on crusade and John's incompetence further weakened this Angevin empire, and within two decades of Henry's death, the relentless ambition of Philip of France had succeeded in regaining all of Normandy, Brittany and much of Aquitaine as the property of the French crown.

Remarkably, Henry had built this empire in the aftermath of civil war in England and Normandy, from the slender base of his father's two counties of Anjou and Maine, and aided by a scattering of supporters elsewhere. What had enabled him to do this was the dire state of England under King Stephen, ravaged by civil war. Henry saw for himself, when he first came to England as a young man, what a disaster a weak king could be, and his passion for law, order and good government arose from his desire to ensure that this should never happen again. When, twenty years later, his sons and some of the great men of the realm rebelled, they were defeated, not by Henry himself, but by his deputies, men whom he had gathered about him who were prepared to support him against powerful enemies. He had chosen them wisely; unlike his grandfather, who employed churchmen in his government, Henry from the outset had sought out literate laymen to carry out his work, men with no other qualifications save intelligence and loyalty to the king's aims.

With the help of such men, Henry's great success lay in the legal and administrative matters of the English royal government. Here he built soundly and well. The English common law as we know it is firmly founded on what he established and his work also survives in the administration of English government.

The picture of Henry's court as a place of lively discussion is the key to his method of working. Henry's objectives, order and justice, were clear enough, and he did not adopt solutions based on theory in order to achieve them. The discussions were between some of the best-educated men in the kingdom, who were also directly involved in implementing Henry's directives in courts and in the king's offices, and the outcome was practical solutions for practical problems. Laws were not arbitrarily handed down by the king; there are frequent references to law being made 'by the advice of the magnates on the authority of the prince'. The councils at Clarendon in 1163 and 1166 were instances of this advice being sought, on an agenda which had already been debated by Henry and his closest councillors.

Henry was interested in making existing systems function better; he was not at heart an innovator – an approach, as we have seen, alien to the medieval mind – but a man who wanted to find better ways of doing things. He and his advisers began with his grandfather's laws and institutions, themselves based on the Norman skill in administration which had emerged a century earlier, and made them the most effective of their kind in Europe.

At the end of Henry's reign, the book that is regarded as the foundation of English 'common' law, the law which applies throughout the land, was compiled by someone with a very detailed knowledge of the subject. Indeed, *The Treatise on the Laws and Customs of the Realm of England* is usually associated with the name of its author and Henry's justiciar, Ranulf de Glanvill himself. Its prologue sets out in sonorous terms the agenda for good government that preoccupied the king and his circle of advisers:

Not only must royal power be furnished with arms against rebels and nations which rise up against the king and the realm, but it is also fitting that it should be adorned with

laws for the governance of subject and peaceful peoples; so
that in time of both peace and war our glorious king may so
successfully perform his office that, crushing the pride of the
unbridled and ungovernable with the right hand of strength
and tempering justice for the humble and meek with the rod
of equity, he may both be always victorious in wars with his
enemies and also show himself continually impartial in dealing with his subjects.[1]

Before Henry's day there were written laws, but the way in
which the law was applied was handed down by word of
mouth. Now there was a general movement towards
recording both how the law should be administered and
also the decisions in particular cases. The 'common law'
was in fact a centralized royal legal system. Many lordships
carried with them the right to hold local courts, from the
manor courts which settled matters relating to a particular
estate to the princely jurisdiction of the bishops of Durham
in their 'palatinate', where royal authority was almost
entirely delegated to them. Henry created a system of justices whose job was to hear both civil and criminal cases,
and who travelled through a specified group of counties;
they also made enquiries about matters on which the king
wanted information. They heard cases that would normally
have been dealt with directly by the king himself, and were
given full personal powers to hold the equivalent of a king's
court. This offered – in theory at least – access to the king's
courts to anyone with a grievance. These royal justices
covered the whole country in their journeys or 'eyres', and
their decisions were mutually binding on the other 'justices

in eyre'. For this purpose, written records of proceedings were kept, unlike at the local courts, where lords and communities were expected to remember the 'customs' and the decisions made there. And any action in the royal court, whether civil, criminal or an inquest, had to be initiated by a written instruction from the king, the 'writ' that is still used today to initiate cases. In certain cases, the use of a jury was introduced, a feature of Anglo-Saxon law courts which had survived in some places in England. It was now made part of the king's justice, and is the origin of the modern jury system. However, in the twelfth century a jury consisted of men from the neighbourhood who knew about the facts of the case already; in other words, they provided evidence rather than listening to it and weighing it up, and were there to assist the sheriff to come to a decision. As to enforcing the judgements in the royal courts, this was delegated to the sheriff of each county. Because the system was carefully adjusted so that it conflicted as little as possible with existing rights to hold local courts, Henry was able to introduce without opposition the novel aspects of the common law. This was in sharp contrast to his lack of success in bringing the Church courts into line with his ideals of justice, where he was faced with the implacable determination of the most powerful organization in medieval Europe to maintain its independence from royal law.

A similar book to *The Treatise on the Laws and Customs of the Realm of England*, on the workings of the Exchequer and the royal finances, *The Dialogue on the Exchequer*, is attributed to Henry's treasurer, Richard fitz Nigel, Archdeacon of Ely. So called from the chequered counting-cloth on which all transactions were carried out, this was a relatively new department of state. In his book Richard sets out the constitution of the Exchequer, and describes its workings; the original version is dated 1177.

At the beginning of Henry's reign, the royal revenues in England were in chaos. Although the system introduced under Henry I for recording the audit of money received from each county continued to be written up, the documents contain everything from simple errors in the mathematics to entries for wholly fictitious counties. We have seen how, nine years after his accession, in 1163, Henry held a major inquiry into the actual state of the nation's finances. The main source of revenue came from the sheriffs, each responsible for the equivalent of a modern county, who paid a fixed sum to the Exchequer annually and then collected the various taxes to which the king was entitled from the inhabitants of the county; any surplus or deficit was the business of the sheriff, and the Exchequer was theoretically guaranteed a definite revenue. The fixed sums, called farms, were negotiated with the sheriff on his appointment, and remained the same until a new sheriff came into office. This meant that raising the fixed sums was a slow business, and two years after the inquiry the revenue from only four farms had been raised. The farms were not always paid on time, and collecting arrears was often difficult. Because of the difficulty of raising royal income, Henry had to reduce the costs of government, and he seems to have succeeded in doing this, as old loans from moneylenders dating from the beginning of the reign were now paid off. The king himself, given the small number of his officials, was closely involved in supervising this kind of official business, and Henry's insistence on good administration was in part a simple necessity to ensure the very survival of the government.

Henry never used the royal revenues for his own personal ends: the simplicity of his own habits and his shunning of ostentation is a consistent theme in the pen-portraits of him that have come down to us. At the end of his reign a chronicler wrote that

> he never laid any grievous burden on his realm of England or on his lands overseas, until the recent tithe for the crusade, which was also levied on other countries. He never laid any tribute on churches or monasteries on pretext of necessity like other monarchs, but even preserved their immunity from tolls with religious fervour. He abhorred bloodshed and the sacrifice of men's lives, and strove diligently to keep the peace, whenever possible by gifts of money but with armed force if he could not secure it otherwise.[2]

That peace was kept in England for the whole of his reign, with the one exception of the invasion of 1173; and he was more successful than his predecessors at controlling the rebellious barons of Normandy and Aquitaine.

In 1767, George Lyttelton wrote the first modern biography of Henry II, proclaiming him at the outset to be 'one of the greatest princes in extent of dominion, in magnanimity, and in abilities that ever governed this nation'.[3] Two and a half centuries later, and after the work of many scholars and much debate, that verdict still stands. Henry may only be remembered now as Becket's nemesis and as the husband of Eleanor of Aquitaine, but it is he, rather than his swashbuckling son Richard, who deserves to have a statue outside the Houses of Parliament, as a king whose influence can still be traced in laws and institutions by which we are governed today.

# Notes

## ABBREVIATIONS

Barber               Richard Barber, *Henry Plantagenet* (Woodbridge: Boydell Press, 2003)
EHD                  *English Historical Documents: Volume II, 1042–1189*, trans. and ed. David Douglas and G. W. Greenaway (London: Eyre & Spottiswoode, 1953)
Fitzstephen          *The Life and Death of Thomas Becket, Chancellor of England and Archbishop of Canterbury, based on the account of William Fitzstephen his clerk, with additions from other contemporary sources*, trans. and ed. George Greenaway (London: Folio Society, 1961)
Warren               W. L. Warren, *Henry II* (London: Eyre Methuen, 1973)
William Marshal      *History of William Marshal*, ed. A. J. Holden, S. Gregory and D. Crouch, Anglo-Norman Text Society, Occasional Publications, Series 4, 3 vols. (London: ANTS, 2002–6)

## I. THE MAN

1. The descriptions are: Walter Map, in *EHD*, pp. 389–90; Peter of Blois, in *Medieval Sourcebook* at http://www.fordham.edu/Halsall/source/1177peterblois-hen2.asp, accessed 24 April 2014; Gerald of Wales, in *EHD*, pp. 386–8.
2. Fitzstephen, p. 46.
3. Fitzstephen, p. 44.
4. Warren, pp. 629–30.
5. Warren, p. 183. John may be echoing a description of rage found in medical textbooks, where illustrations show victims of rage throwing off their clothes and chewing them.
6. Warren, p. 509.
7. Gerald of Wales, in *EHD*, p. 387.
8. Warren, p. 209.
9. Walter Map, in *EHD*, p. 390.
10. Gerald of Wales, in *EHD*, p. 387.
11. Gerald of Wales, in *EHD*, p. 388.
12. *Peterborough Chronicle*, entry for the year 1137 (author's translation).
13. C. Warren Hollister, *Henry I* (New Haven, Conn., and London: Yale University Press, 2001), p. 497.
14. Walter Map, in *EHD*, p. 390.

15. Barber, p. 44.
16. Gerald of Wales, in *EHD*, pp. 387–8.
17. Warren, p. 587.
18. Gerald of Wales, in Warren, p. 592.
19. Roger of Howden, in Warren p. 592.
20. T. A. Archer, 'Clifford, Rosamund (*b.* before 1140?, *d.* 1175/6)', rev. Elizabeth Hallam, *Oxford Dictionary of National Biography* (Oxford: Oxford University Press, 2004); also at http://www.oxforddnb.com.ezproxy.londonlibrary.co.uk/view/article/5661, accessed 22 April 2014.

# 2. HIS STORY

1. Barber, p. 49.
2. Henry of Huntingdon, in *EHD*, p. 313.
3. Fitzstephen, p. 48.
4. Barber, p. 102.
5. Fitzstephen, p. 51.
6. Z. N. Brooke, *The English Church and the Papacy from the Conquest to the Reign of John* (Cambridge: Cambridge University Press, 1931), p. 193.
7. Barber, p. 110.
8. *EHD*, p. 722.
9. *EHD*, p. 725n.
10. *EHD*, p. 732.
11. Fitzstephen, p. 128.
12. Barber, p. 137.
13. Ibid.
14. Polydore Vergil, *Polydori Vergilii Anglicae Historiae Libri Vigintisex* (Basel: Michael Isingrin, 1545), pp. 215–16 (author's translation).
15. Fitzstephen, p. 137n.
16. Fitzstephen, p. 140.
17. *EHD*, p. 758.
18. Fitzstephen, p. 146n.
19. Gervase of Canterbury, *The Historical Works of Gervase of Canterbury*, ed. William Stubbs, Rolls Series, 2 vols. (London: Longman Green, 1879–80), vol. 1, p. 219.
20. Fitzstephen, p. 163.
21. Warren, pp. 532–3.
22. *William Marshal*, vol. 1, ll. 7038–155.
23. Gerald of Wales, *Giraldi Cambrensis Opera*, ed. J. S. Brewer, J. F. Dimock and F. Warner, Rolls Series, 8 vols. (London: Longman Green, 1861–91), vol. 8, p. 233 (author's translation).
24. *William Marshal*, vol. 1, ll. 8843–44.
25. Gerald of Wales, in *EHD*, p. 384.
26. Ibid.
27. *William Marshal*, vol. 1, ll. 9293–303.

## 3. HIS ACHIEVEMENTS

1. *The Treatise on the Laws and Customs of the Realm of England Commonly Called Glanvill*, ed. G. D. G. Hall (Oxford: Oxford University Press, 1993), p. 1.
2. William of Newburgh, in *EHD*, pp. 372–3.
3. George Lyttelton, *The History of the Life of King Henry the Second*, 5 vols. (London: Sandby and Dodsley, 1767–72), vol. 1, p. i.

# Further Reading

W. L. Warren's *Henry II* (London: Eyre Methuen, 1973), in the English Monarchs series, is still the standard biography: it is very substantial, and although parts of it have been superseded by more recent research, it is still largely in tune with current thinking. My own *Henry Plantagenet*, published eight years earlier, is the most recent popular biography (London: Barrie and Rockliff with Pall Mall Press, 1964; reissued Woodbridge: Boydell Press, 2003), which is both surprising and puzzling. On the scholarly side *Henry II: New Interpretations*, edited by Christopher Harper-Bill and Nicholas Vincent (Woodbridge: Boydell Press, 2007), covers the extensive work done since W. L. Warren's book first appeared. New research on the reign of Henry II is covered by the annual Battle Conference and published each year as *Anglo-Norman Studies* (Woodbridge: Boydell Press, 1979– ).

Thomas Becket and Eleanor of Aquitaine have both proved more attractive subjects for biographers than Henry himself. In addition to John Guy's highly praised *Thomas Becket: Warrior, Priest, Rebel, Victim* (London: Viking, 2012), there is Frank Barlow's distinguished account, *Thomas Becket* (London: Weidenfeld & Nicolson, 1986). Eleanor, rather than Henry himself, is the favourite topic for popular books on the Plantagenets. On Eleanor of Aquitaine, Alison Weir gives a highly readable account of her in *Eleanor of Aquitaine: By the Wrath of God, Queen of England* (London: Jonathan Cape, 1999), while Régine Pernoud's *Eleanor of Aquitaine* (London: Collins, 1967) is the work of a very distinguished French historian. Ralph Turner's *Eleanor of Aquitaine: Queen of France, Queen of England* (New Haven, Conn.: Yale University Press, 2009) concentrates on the historical evidence, stripping away the modern romantic overlay from her story.

There are no complete modern translations of the major chronicles of Henry's reign, but much material on Becket is available: *The Lives of Thomas Becket*, translated by Michael Staunton (Manchester: Manchester University Press, 2001), covers the major biographies written in the years immediately following his death. A translation is included in the very expensive Oxford Medieval Texts edition of Walter Map's *De Nugis Curialium: Courtiers' Trifles*, edited by M. R. James and revised by C. N. L. Brooke and R. A. B. Mynors (Oxford: Clarendon Press, 1983). *The Autobiography of Gerald of Wales* has been translated by H. E. Butler (London: Jonathan Cape, 1937). And the descriptions of Henry II by Gerald of Wales and Peter of Blois are translated in *English Historical Documents: Volume II, 1042–1189*, edited by David Douglas and G. W. Greenaway (London: Eyre & Spottiswoode, 1953), with some excerpts from the chronicles of the period.

# Picture Credits

1. Scenes from the life of King Saul, illuminated manuscript from Winchester, by the Master of the Morgan Leaf, *c.*1160–80 (The Pierpont Morgan Library, New York, © 2014. Pierpont Morgan Library/Art Resource/Scala, Florence)

2. Enamel plaque for the tomb of Geoffrey Plantagenet, from the Cathedral of St Julien, Le Mans, *c.*1151–5 (Musée de Tessé, Le Mans/Bridgeman Images)

3. Effigies of Plantagenet royalty at Fontevraud Abbey, France (Bridgeman Images)

4. Depiction of Henry II and Eleanor of Aquitaine from the east window of Poitiers Cathedral, late twelfth century (Cathedral of St Pierre, Poitiers/akg-images/Bildarchiv Monheim GmbH)

5. Becket departs from Louis VII and Henry II in January 1169, from the Becket Leaves manuscript, English School, *c.*1220–40 (The Wormsley Library/Bridgeman Images)

6. The coronation of Henry the young king, from the Becket Leaves manuscript, English School, *c.*1220–40 (The Wormsley Library/Bridgeman Images)

7. Eleanor of Aquitaine out hawking, thirteenth-century fresco in the Chapel of St Radegund, Chinon (De Agostini Picture Library/Bridgeman Images)

8. Enamel plaque depicting Henry of Blois, shown presenting an altar to an unknown church, probably made in England *c.*1150–71 (© The Trustees of the British Museum, London)

9. Thirteenth-century stained-glass window showing Henry II at the tomb of Thomas Becket, Trinity Chapel, Canterbury Cathedral, Kent (Bridgeman Images)

# Index